The Golden Rules of Economics

PETER M. VESSENES

DEDICATION

This is the third edition of this book. With the election over, and with many requests for continuing the message in this book to others by readers, I have gone through revising The Golden Rules to make it a bit more timely.

Many thanks are in place. There are so many people who have made incredible sacrifices to bring this book about in time for the election. Every one of them deserves an outstanding measure of gratitude.

First to my editors, which include Jamie Quanrud, Kelly Henry, Steve Quanrud, and my BFF and wife, Katherine Vessenes. Without your critical eyes (and some disagreements about style...) the book would never have been finished.

Without the outstanding team of people who helped create and validate the cites that are the basis for my observations throughout the book, The Golden Rules of Economics would have been lacking in the TRUTH so necessary to overcome the flawed talking points drilled into our heads from so many quarters in today's society. In addition to my editors above, my thanks go out to Josh Lantz, Maureen McNeal, P. Revere, Jill Fredrickson, Ann Belden, Paul Quanrud, and his wife Donna Quanrud.

A special thanks to Dr. Richard Skoog and Joseph Henry for help on the health care and banking sections of this book. Deep appreciation for your extra work.

A singular thanks to Kassandra Kuehl for her tireless efforts with Kevin Deshler and his outstanding team at Risdall Marketing Group.

Finally, special appreciation to Paul Quanrud and his brother, Steve Quanrud, for managing the layout of the book in preparation for publishing in record time.

My apologies to anyone I might have left out. I appreciate all of your sacrifices.

Most importantly, the true dedication of all of our efforts go out to you, our readers.

We are facing a very serious set of decisions on the part of Congress, the White House, and state governments over the next 10 years. The consequences of how American citizens hold their elected officials accountable will be with us for the next 25 years. If they will not take the real steps to protect the Golden Rules of Economics we must continue to replace them with people who will in each election cycle. This is a real war. It has be aggressively waged against us since Teddy Roosevelt and Woodrow Wilson and continued relentlessly through Barak Husain Obama. We cannot survive if we allow politicians to continue making the wrong choices.

I trust this book, and the things you will learn from it, will give you a clearer understanding of how our nation has gotten to the state it is in today. May it show you how to share it with others, and provide the motivation and drive to rise up like the patriots of the American Revolution to put down the economic tyranny that threatens our country and established the real way both an economy and a free nation should operate.

Enjoy the read!

THE GOLDEN RULES OF ECONOMICS

CONTENTS

PREFACE

The United States has been in turmoil since I was a teenager. Many aspects of life in our country have taken the nation to great levels of conflict and trauma. These have ranged from the day I listened to Martin Luther King, when he walked through my hometown on the South Side of Chicago (and was shocked to find out how many of my high school peers were abject racists), to the college friends who died in Vietnam, to the wild and loose sexual morals of those times, to the magnitude of "social" drug use, from pot to LSD, and on to the numbers of college professors I met who knew little of the real world.

I was fortunate. In high school I was one of a select 30 junior year students who participated in a class labeled "Creative Learning Processes." The class met two hours a day, every day, as a substitute for English and Social Studies. The heads of each department, Mr. Mackie and Mr. Edwards, taught the class. We called it the "Macwards" class, but it was only years later I fully grasped the consequences of that educational experience.

This class began by forcing us to take massively extensive notes on 90-minute lectures by each teacher. The topics had little to do with English or Social Studies, but seemed topics of interest to the teachers. Each week, we turned in our notes, received grades back – but the notes, (or rational for the grade) were never returned.

This was followed by weeks of being assigned research on very specific topics. The information was usually not available in the school library, and in those days there was no Internet. Pages upon pages of research were compiled, turned in, graded, and never returned.

By this time many in the class were wondering why on earth they agreed to be part of the program. We survived on discipline, and were even allowed to assign ourselves grades (most of us got an "A"), but there was as much conversation about "what is going on" as there was about the topics we were studying. Mackie and Edwards never said a word, despite frequent questions, both in class and privately...

Finally, the class got fun. We were put in teams of five people each. Each was asked to research a topic, put together a presentation using multi-media,

i

and give a presentation to the rest of the class. Mackie and Edwards assigned the teams, and we were on our own. We were also to be graded on a "curve," but were never told the criteria for grading, or given comments for "improving" what we were doing.

The class culminated with each team competing against one other on assessing a relevant social/political issue of the time. This occurred five times, so each team could work against each other team, but we were assigned which "side" we were to prove. We did not get to choose to prove and defend what we personally believed in.

By this time, I knew the program's objective. I, and anyone who stayed disciplined, had been trained to be a "world class" objective thinker with growing presentation and persuasion skills. Later in my life it allowed me to become a "think tank" facilitator.

The following year, as part of the program, I was asked to become part of a team of five seniors who went into the Chicago Inner City High School system to evaluate those schools. I wound up as the natural leader of the team, giving presentations of our findings to teachers, administrators, and parent-teacher organizations.

My brain was addicted to how my problem solving and thinking processes had been trained. Every political, economic, and social issue of the day became an obsession.

I couldn't help it; I learned how people could come to flawed conclusions, and what caused them. I learned how the media and education shaped beliefs rather than presented facts and information, and how to leave the "belief" side to editorial pages and personal commentary. I learned how social groups banded together to either protect themselves or gain power over others. I saw first-hand how beliefs were always more powerful than the truth, and emotions always over-ruled sound reasoning and logic.

The most important thing I learned? When boiled down to the most basic terms, the fundamental core items were always the same.

1. What must happen to survive
2. What must happen to have provision (food, clothing, shelter)

3.   What must happen to escape the oppression, pain, trauma

What is the root of all of these items? Money, or the lack of it.

A quick cruise through our nation's history proves this. The American Revolution was a war against economic oppression from Great Britain and King George. The Civil War was a war tipping on the economic dependence of the South on slave labor.

Hitler's rise to power in post-World War I resulted from Progressive economic theories inflicted on Germany by United States university economics professors. These theories did not work, and the massive devaluation and inflation of Germany in the 1930s triggered Hitler's rise to power.

The relative "peace and prosperity" of the 1950s was a result of the rest of the industrial world being so devastated by World War II that the United States prospered by being the only "modern" nation not struck by the war on its own soil. We rose as the standard of the world in manufacturing, and the ensuing balance of trade advantage we held by being the world's largest exporter with no real competitors, created great wealth in our nation.

We have reached the time where "Progressive" economic policies will soon leave us in a state similar to Germany in the 1930s. There are many examples of this occurring even in today's world. Greece is at the brink of total collapse[i] after 35 years of Socialism and the theft of larger private businesses by the Greek government during that time. Argentina's inflation rate is so high and fast that wages are upgraded weekly to account for the collapse of the Argentinean currency.[ii]

There are many concerns we face in America today. They include different beliefs and opinions on women's rights and abortion; whether federal, state, and local employees should be unionized; separation of Church and State; whether marriage is legal between two different genders or not, and many other issues. Our country is a great place that allows us to discuss, dissect, endorse or refute these and many other thoughts and beliefs that impact our lives. These disagreements are not allowed in Totalitarian or Sharia Law Islamic countries.

This book is not about any of those issues. We face a far more critical crisis. We are near the tipping point of the largest Economic War in global history, and there is a short time to fix it.

If we do not fix the money disaster we are hurtling towards at breakneck speed, there will not be the place, time, or opportunity to solve these concerns and our other differences. Without fixing this crisis now we will be left in the same places Germany descended to in the late 1930s and 1940s, or a takeover by a despot, much like Venezuela, or total economic collapse like Greece or Argentina.

Today, let us agree on what threatens our survival today – you see, after all:

"It is all about the money, and we are not stupid...

THE GOLDEN RULES OF ECONOMICS

1 THE GOLDEN RULES OF ECONOMICS

Life has many Golden Rules. There are many reasons they are "Golden." They can create fulfilling, healthy friendships and families. They can provide standards by which each of us live our lives, for making ethical and moral day-to-day decisions we believe in. They allow us to "love ourselves," and love others the way we want to be loved. They allow us to create a set of "rules" by which we live our lives. Perhaps the best known Golden Rule is, "He who has the Gold makes the Rules."

The foundation of The United States of America was born out of this "Golden Rule." Business and commerce in the original 13 colonies out-performed Great Britain. As a result, Great Britain and King George were seeing less gold. We liked the rules of free trade and ability to reward ourselves without government stealing our prosperity. When this rule was violated, the American Revolution was born.

I have written this book from a lifetime of professional and personal obsessive dedication to recognizing when things are wrong, finding out how they got broken, and figuring out how to fix them. During the national election of 2008 I saw our country headed down a terrible path; one that must change or we would be broken forever. Both before and since then, so many Golden Rules have been violated that the future of our country, and by that most of the world, hangs in the balance.

We cannot be naïve. Not all people are "moral, ethical, and righteous." The laws and regulations in government are supposed to protect its citizens from individuals and organizations who follow practices that destroy the foundational premise of our Constitution:

We the People of the United States, in Order to form a more perfect Union, establish Justice, insure Domestic Tranquility, provide for the Common Defense, promote the General Welfare and secure the Blessings of Liberty to ourselves and our posterity do ordain and establish this Constitution for the United States of America.

The challenge occurs when someone's survival is threatened; they will do whatever they think necessary to avoid death or torture. In fact, people must believe their own personal survival, safety, and continuing needs are secure *before* they can extend a helping hand. Never forget, the Good Samaritan had money! People need to believe there is a playing field with rules enforced so they can pursue their personal welfare.

Today we are faced with a society that has lost touch with most of The Golden Rules of Economics. Why are The Golden Rules of Economics so important? Without knowing them, understanding them, enforcing them, and living by them, our nation will descend into the poverty of Third World Nations, and get caught in the looming financial bankruptcy of the European Economic Community.[iii]

Both Liberals and Conservatives believe they are "fighting" to bring about a better way of life and a better economy. Neither side has national economic collapse as part of their political agenda. Unfortunately, not many in either political party or their leaders seem to understand the most basic building blocks of The Golden Rules of Economics. I have written this book to create a clear understanding of those Rules.

The Rules are not arbitrary. In fact most of them are instinctive to us as human beings, and the rest are easy to understand through history, current events, and our own life experiences. I have not written this book to gain a Ph.D. in Economics from the University of Chicago. The book was written so regular American citizens of every social, economic, national and racial background can understand the real Rules.

The book is not a mere "solo" effort. Incredible contributions from many members of TrueCapitalism (http://truecapitalism.org/), Katherine (my best friend and wife for 37 years), and many other outstanding individuals with as much experience in politics as I have in business turnarounds made this book possible. Without their continued help, counsel, research, efforts and encouragement this book would never have come about.

I have tried to write in a way that can be heard above the usual political talking points and other din so prevalent in Presidential election years. The Golden Rules must stand against all traditional, emotional, and irrational arguments hurled by Progressives, Liberals, Democrats and "Inside the

Beltway" Republicans.[iv] Even listening to most conservative commentators drives me a little batty; I am not interested in language and talking points that only conservatives understand. We have to bring clarity to all citizens. It is not always easy, as the people we most need to persuade have faulty underlying beliefs. These "beliefs" create powerful negative emotions, and keep them from seeing The Golden Rules.

This is no small challenge. Faulty beliefs are indoctrinated at an early age in the general population, and reinforced by mainstream media (both news and entertainment) and our educational systems. Add to this political talking points, and policies created and enforced by administration regulatory agencies outside the jurisdiction of Congress, and you have a chilling effect on The United States.

We must defeat this at its roots. I hope this book can show you by your own life experiences the REAL Golden Rules, even if they are *contrary* to your beliefs.

After all, if they are Golden Rules, they are irrefutably The Truth.

THE GOLDEN RULES OF ECONOMICS

2 THE GOLDEN RULES OF ECONOMICS IN PEOPLE

Golden Rules should be learned very early in life. My third grade teacher, Miss Lehman, taught me one of the most important.

One Saturday my mother could not find a babysitter for my younger brother John and me. A Depression-era baby, mom would visit her Uncle George each month to pick up food from his distribution company, Phillips Jams and Jellies. There we were, overwhelmed by the size of great Uncle George's company when he leaned over to me and asked, "Peter, do you want half a dollar?" "Yes Uncle George, thank you." "Johnny, do you want half a dollar?" "Uh huh!"

Uncle George pulled out his wallet, removed a one dollar bill, ripped it in half, and gave each of us a piece. My mother went ballistic.

"George, what are you doing??? Give me those!!! I will scotch tape them!!! How could you do that??? I will give you quarters!!! Don't you DARE spend that money!!!"

The ranting went on several minutes. Needless to say, I could not get the event out of my head, and so at the end of Vocabulary Class on Monday, I stuck up my hand (accompanied by groans from my classmates...).

"Miss Lehman, could you explain the definition of 'money'?"

I was just 9 years old, and had no idea what money was, or why it would cause my mother to go crazy in front of Uncle George and his employees. Miss Lehman jumped on this instantly.

"Peter, what a great question! We are going to learn a couple of new vocabulary words!" (More groans).

Miss Lehman went on to ask questions of the class:

"How many of your daddies build cars?" There was a Ford plant near our community.

"How many of your daddies and mommies make Cracker Jack?" Also nearby…

"How many of your daddies build houses?"

"How many of your mommies plant gardens or make clothing by sewing?"

"Does anyone's daddy sell medicine?" Stan's dad owned the Rexall Drugstore in town…

And so on until she had named every parent's occupation in the class.

Then she asked Stan, "Can your daddy build or fix a car?" "Oh no Miss Lehman, he tried once, and mommy said NEVER TO DO IT AGAIN!"

Another question, "Sally, your mommy is an excellent gardener, does she grow all the food you eat?" "Oh no Miss Lehman, I go with her to the grocery store all the time."

On and on went the questions until she established that none of our parents could create or produce all the things we used and lived with. She went on to explain, "Long ago, people used to trade what they were good at, or could do, with other people who had things or help they needed." That brought us to our first new vocabulary word.

Barter

She then went on to say that as transportation through trains, buses, trucks, cars and airplanes grew that people much farther away could trade what they had with others that did not live in their neighborhoods. Because it was not practical to trade your mother's strawberries for a pair of shoes made in Milwaukee, money became a method of valuing each item in the trade.

At last I understood what money was, but Miss Lehman was not done. "That leads us to our second vocabulary word, '**Capitalism.**'"

She spelled it on the chalkboard, had us write it down, and had us say it out loud. Then she gave us the definition of Capitalism:

"Capitalism is a system of Barter in which all the trading partners believe they are receiving equal or greater value in exchange for what they gave up. Write it down."

There we were; the definition was on the chalkboard, we were writing it down, and then she had us say it out loud. Next came the biggest surprise.

"More than this, Capitalism is not a theory; it is instinctive – you do it every day!"

Out of the back of the room, Charlie, a baseball fanatic and the tough kid in the class (remember, this is the South Side of Chicago) jumped up and said,

"I don't do no STINKIN' CAPITALISM."

"Yes you do!"

"NO I DON'T!"

"YES YOU DO!"

"NO I DON'T"

"How much is a Mickey Mantle Card worth?"

"TWO DUKE SNYDERS."

It hit the room like a ton of bricks. We DID understand Barter, and it was instinctive. I discovered at 9 years old that the real definition of Capitalism was wired into us as a creature, and there was no escaping it.

Many things play into Capitalism and affect our lives through it. In college, I discovered another very important piece...

Abraham Maslow discovered and documented a hierarchy of needs in his 1943 paper, *A Theory of Human Motivation.*[v] His theories parallel many other theories of human <u>developmental psychology</u>, all of which focus on the stages of growth in people. Maslow's theory is more fully explained and developed in his 1954 book, *Motivation and Personality.*

The following graph is a simplified version of Maslow's theory:

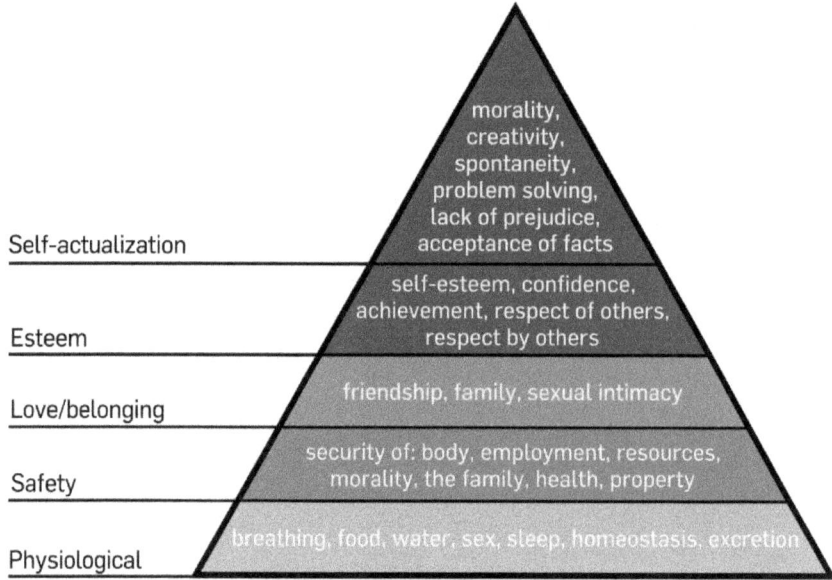

Once we look past the Physiological needs, we see four key elements. These are:

1. *Safety* – Predicated on survival, protection, health, food, shelter and so on...
2. *Love/Belonging* – Where friendship, family, social groups, and so on, come into play.
3. *Esteem* – Where personal self-worth resides; people become confident, they believe in their achievements, they respect others, and become respected by others.
4. *Self-Actualization* – Where the true "outward" focus of our lives takes place. Lack of prejudice, acceptance of facts, problem solving, and

so on, put us in a role of contributing back to society and life. This phase builds life purpose and generates personal growth.

Today, the accumulation of faulty policies, flawed underlying beliefs, and violations of instinctive behavior in people have left the vast majority of the United States population not feeling "Safe." This has been reflected in several ways: the high percentage of people who believe the country is heading in the wrong direction, lack of confidence in President Obama, and extremely low confidence ratings in Congress.

The challenge we face is that once Safety is eroded, the higher levels and purposes in life (Love/Belonging, Esteem, Self-Actualization) cannot be fulfilled. This is one of the underlying causes of our economy's – and ultimately our society's – collapse.

The Truth about Basic Human Rights

Let's start with some core principles: Just because you are born into the world does not mean you are "owed" food, clothing or shelter.

Most parents love their children. The basic human drive to provide these fundamental needs to a child is instinctive in all people who are not psychologically imbalanced. Part of growing up is discovering your unique skills, disciplines, perseverance, knowledge and abilities.

The objective is to find a way to provide for **you**. Like it or not this is a basic TRUTH of life, irrespective of the social, political, or economic system under which you live. You may have gone to college because it was "the thing to do," or "to party" or "to find a spouse." You should have gone to college to better discover who you are and build a career – in other words, to partially come out from under your parents' wings.

It is easy to understand why young adults can fall into feeling entitled. They have been protected and provided for throughout their entire lives. Most did not enter adulthood expecting to have to care and provide for themselves. They did not pursue a career-focused educational or vocational path. They grew up in a time of "bounty." They believe they have a "higher moral ground" in Maslow's Theory. No wonder Francois Guizot said,

"A young man who is not a liberal has no heart, but an old man who is not a conservative has no brains…"

The Golden Rules of Economics in People

- The true definition of Capitalism is a system of Barter in which all the trading partners believe they are receiving equal or greater value in exchange for what they gave up.
- The true definition of Capitalism is instinctive in every single living soul whether we recognize it or not.
- Each person must make a valuable contribution to his community in order to provide for his own basic needs (Safety).
- People are only owed the **right** to pursue an opportunity that may come along. They do not have the right to demand an opportunity, only the **right** to pursue opportunities without bias or prejudice.
- People have the right to engage in trade with others if they so choose.
- It is the responsibility of parents and schools to educate children in these Truths.
- It is the responsibility of communities and government to protect people's rights to pursue opportunity.
- There is NO guarantee any opportunity pursued will be fulfilled.

This is the story of life. We pursue opportunities, we discover which we can fulfill, and from this we live and fulfill our lives.

3 THE GOLDEN RULES OF ECONOMICS IN CAPITALISM

Life is a very complex composite of skills, disciplines, abilities and cooperation. No man stands alone, not even a hermit. Basic needs include:

- Raising and harvesting food
- Creating tools
- Creating clothing
- Building shelter
- Creating and harvesting sources of energy (warmth)

No one can generate all these items alone. Even the hermit needed the person who crafted his axe or knife, the iron refinery that supplied the steel for the blade, and the store where the knife was acquired. Trading for our needs is a basic element of survival as a species.

People start trading as children. Trading toys, baseball cards, and time on a favorite activity, are as natural to children as being self-centered, learning new words, and whining when they don't get what they want.

People also instinctively sense what they believe is "fair" in a trade. Fundamentally, people only move ahead on a trade when they believe they have received equal or greater value in exchange for what they gave up. Applying this to all parties in a trade, we come to a fundamental statement describing an instinctive behavior:

People only engage in trading when everyone who is trading believes they receive equal or greater value in exchange for what they gave up in the trade.

If we modify this statement slightly, we get back to the TRUE definition of Capitalism:

An Economic System of Barter (Trading) in which all the Trading Parties Believe They Receive Equal or Greater Value in Exchange for what they Gave Up.

In fact Capitalism is INSTINCTIVE, and some skill in trade is *critical* to reach even the level of Safety in Maslow's *Theory of Human Motivation.*

Even people who believe they are owed the basics of life participate in true Capitalism. They make daily decisions about the clothes they wear, which cell phones they use, whether they are Mac or PC, and so on.

Note that there is a hidden word in the true definition of Capitalism; that word is "**believe.**"

Some people are very good at getting others to believe in the value of the trade. We have words to describe them:

Con Man   Grifter   Charlatan   Enron   Madoff

Among the most important roles of government are establishing laws and regulations that help protect people from scam artists; delivering consequences to the guilty; and when possible, providing relief to their victims. This is why it is important for people to learn at an early age how to engage in smart trading; that is, **Smart Capitalism**.

It is not, and never will be, government's role to make sure all trades are **fair.** This results in the kind of governmental sleight of hand created in the Truman presidency,[vi] when the administration regulated most major industries' prices in the name of National Security. Fortunately, most of these controls were removed during the Reagan presidency.[vii]

The worst possible situation occurs when government believes it is in the best interest of its people to remove free trade. This was the old Soviet Union. They controlled every aspect of life, leaving the individual with almost no choices. Removal of choice destroyed the human spirit, and led to many horrid conditions including depression, self-medication and addiction (alcohol), and Gulags or death for dissenters.

As people get better at trading, they become more successful. Self-interest prevails, though many people build ways of packaging themselves to others (and even to themselves) in an attempt to avoid appearing selfish. We call this *The Façade*, and until people hit Self-actualization in Maslow's model they remain in a primarily self-serving state.

This description of mankind's condition is not an accusation; it is factually the way life occurs. When large numbers of people are constantly forced into trades they fundamentally know are not "fair," there are significant consequences.

The Truth about Violating Capitalism

All of us have been involved in a trade for which we later find out someone got the better of us. Maybe we even knew it when it was happening, if we were pushed to a point of desperation. Hopefully, few of us have been pillaged by the Bernie Madoffs of the world.

When trading is consistently unfair, several things are certain:
- People grow unmotivated in their work. "Why should I work quickly and efficiently for the same pay as my co-worker who is slow, sloppy, and will never lose his job?"
- The quality of products and services falls.
- Less money is made by businesses, as the delivery of their goods and services grows inferior.
- Hiring stops; layoffs increase.
- The general economy slows.
- Companies go out of business.

The Golden Rules of Economics in Capitalism

- Oppressing Capitalism in humans has terrible long-term consequences.
- Government's responsibility is to provide a level playing field for the instinctive nature of Capitalism to thrive in a society.
- Being cheated in Capitalism by government or "con artists" or monopolies destroys strong economies, the quality of life, and the spirit of humanity.

13

THE GOLDEN RULES OF ECONOMICS

4 THE GOLDEN RULES OF ECONOMICS IN MERCANTILISM

The American Revolution against Great Britain was an incredible historical event. It was not the first revolution against a parent government, and not the first against oppression of personal liberty. The uniqueness of the American Revolution is that it was a war against economic oppression by Great Britain.

Although the Founding Fathers had many differences in their beliefs about the role of government in the lives of its citizens, what they had in common was understanding those parts of human nature that conspire to create oppressive governments.

The basic cause of the American Revolution was that American entrepreneurs began to out-compete their British counterparts. This meant less money for the King and his Parliament, and England suffered economically in both their import/export businesses, (the basis for financial survival of the British Empire), and their government.

Great Britain had many colonies around the world. These came about by being captured by the British military and populated by British citizens. These colonies became part of a feeder system of raw materials, goods, and services to build the empire and provide economic advantage to England and the Crown.

This was sustained by England providing "favor" to shipping and import/export companies that "paid" for the privilege of limited competition. Unfortunately for King George, the upstart Americans refused to abide by these rules and instead engaged in what they believed were fair trades for their efforts.

In retaliation, American shipping vessels were labeled pirates, boarded and ransacked by British naval ships. The ultimate indignation occurred when the King proclaimed excessive taxes on goods imported by the American colonies. This triggered the Boston Tea Party, and with a cry of *"Taxation without Representation,"* the American Revolution began.

When the Founding Fathers crafted the Constitution and three branches of government, their purpose was singular: Limit government's ability to control the economy to the advantage of a few. Our Congress, Administration, and Judiciary were structured to avoid how Great Britain crippled the American colonies economically, while our Constitution provides all citizens an equal OPPORTUNITY to build their own lives and prosper.

In the 19th Century, the collusion between government and business to provide unfair advantage to a few businesses while strengthening the power of those in government was called Mercantilism.

It is critical to understand that Mercantilism is not Capitalism. Capitalism is *an economic system of trade in which all trading partners believe they receive equal or greater value in exchange for what they give up.* Mercantilism, however, deliberately gives unequal advantage and privilege to some businesses while providing power and privilege to those in government.

By its very nature, Mercantilism creates a ruling class. The "rulers" are those in powerful positions in government, or very high up in a business or other organizations (think unions and union leadership) that is given unearned advantages by government so it can provide politicians and bureaucrats with money and power.

Ruling class economics have existed since medieval feudalism. In a feudal system, all land is owned by the king. Dukes, barons, and princes manage the land through work of serfs, to the advantage of the king and ruling class.

Today there are politicians, both Democrat and Republican, who make up the ruling class. There are individuals in large business, banking and finance who make up the ruling class. Others in manufacturing, labor unions, higher education and national defense make up the ruling class. Individuals in mainstream media make up the ruling class.

This is truly "insider politics." The ruling class works inside politics to maintain their power and money, undermining fair opportunity. It is an economic system designed to minimize or ignore anyone in a trade who is not

16

part of the ruling class or paying for the privilege of being awarded taxpayer dollars.

What is the outcome? The ruling class plays insider, crony politics to Undermine Fair Opportunity – the real UFO of our day. It is not Economics. It is Kleptonomics – *Klepto* in Greek meaning *to steal.*

How has this been done the past 50 years?

First, the ruling class and mainstream media ignore the true definition of Capitalism. If you think I am kidding, try asking anyone you know, "What is the true definition of Capitalism?" I have asked high-ranking conservative Republicans who have served in our government, and they could not define it! Instead, the ruling class obscures the real definition.

The ruling class and mainstream media redefine Capitalism with phrases like *"the rich get richer."* Then the mainstream media and politicians tie the abuses of ruling class businesses and their collusion with government into the definition of Capitalism: *"Of course it is unfair… look at what ("big company") has done! They should not be paying themselves millions off the back of Main Street Americans!"*

The way I learned the real definition of Capitalism exposes the sad story of today's educational system. It was 1959 in my third grade class when I asked Miss Lehmann, "What is money?" By the time she was done she had said, "Even we third graders practice Capitalism every day." This was not hard to understand; every boy in my class knew that one Mickey Mantle Baseball Card was worth two Duke Snyder's in a trade…

How terrible that the very thing that brought about the American Revolution is in today's Washington Government. This is today's Mercantilism. It is *Washington Inc.*

The Golden Rules of Economics in Mercantilism
- Washington Inc. is NOT Capitalism.
- Washington Inc. is Kleptonomics.

17

THE GOLDEN RULES OF ECONOMICS

5 THE GOLDEN RULES OF ECONOMICS IN PROGRESSIVES AND LIBERALS

Since the days of Teddy Roosevelt, through the days of Franklin D. Roosevelt (FDR) and Lyndon B. Johnson (LBJ) and finally culminating with Barak Obama, many Progressives carry a core set of beliefs that shape their view of the world. Let's be very clear: Beliefs are stronger than the Truth.

Let me repeat that – **People's personal beliefs are stronger than the truth.**

If you need simple evidence, consider how a culture could take young men and women and brainwash them. What do they brainwash them to do? They believe that wearing a suicide belt to mass murder large groups of people who do not share their religious beliefs brings a promise of "Pleasing God, with Great Rewards Awaiting You In the Afterlife…"

It is important that everyone understands others' core beliefs. From this we can find out how those beliefs fundamentally violate not only The Golden Rules of Economics, but also the instinctive truths of mankind.

Though not meant as a comprehensive view of Progressives, the following are seven core beliefs they all carry:

1. *Equality for All*
From a Progressive/Liberal perspective it is more important that everyone has an equal piece of the pie rather than the chance to succeed or not. This leads to sacrificing freedoms and the chance to pursue personal goals, all while making sure everyone is pursuing the same end result and is equipped with the same tools. In Canada, a new rule has been adopted in a children's soccer league that says any team winning a game by more than five points will lose by default. The truth is that a society without the ability to succeed or fail ultimately fails. Liberty has been sacrificed for the notion of equality. Everything gets equalized, nothing is outstanding and nothing is superior.

2. *Belief in Big Government*

Those who believe in large government with invasive rules and regulations do not trust individuals to make decisions in everyone's **collective** best interest. After all, they reason, how could selfishly driven people who are better than others at trading serve the best interest of everyone? They believe government is capable of minimizing such trades, and government regulating in the best interest of the people achieves a "fair" result.

3. *Controlled or Regulated Markets*

To "protect" everyone, the government must exert control to force compliance with standards set by government oversight. Personally, I do believe not all standards are wrong or detrimental. Health and safety standards such as homogenizing milk make perfect sense, as long as the government does not "outlaw" raw milk from those who choose to provide or purchase it. On the other hand, think of the Food & Drug Administration (FDA) and the recent banning of CFCs in albuterol.[viii] The change was made regarding the "damaging" impact to the ozone layer of <u>trace</u> amounts of these chlorofluorocarbons in the pressuring system of asthma inhalers. As of January 1, 2012, you can only get prescription inhalers for asthma relief. The price went up from about $17 to $40 per inhaler as a result of the CFC ban.[ix] Three million asthmatics are affected by this regulation.

4. *The Redistribution of Wealth Will Bring Happiness*

Progressives believe if you are not reaching "an acceptable standard of living," (which they believe they can determine), then it is up to government to provide it for you. Progressives give many reasons why such an "imbalance" occurs. These include racial and other forms of discrimination, language barriers, lack of diversity... The rationalizations are almost endless.

It is CRITICAL that government, as much as possible, creates a level playing field of **opportunity**. Racial discrimination is a horrid condition, and thrusts the victims - "discriminated against parties" - into terrible circumstances. Fundamentally, it limits their ability to fulfill their instinctive drive regarding Capitalism.

It is NOT GOVERNMENT'S JOB to force level results in trade. This merely violates one or more of the trading partners' ability in Capitalism, leading to worse results than merely someone in the trade coming out better than another.

Benjamin Franklin had an understanding regarding the ability of money to deliver satisfaction to a person's life. He stated, *"Money never made a man happy yet, nor will it. The more a man has, the more he wants. Instead of filling a vacuum, it makes one."*[x] If money without earned success does not bring happiness, then redistributing money won't make for a happier America. The key to happiness is through success, as opposed to simply getting more money. The goal of our government should be to give all Americans the greatest opportunity possible to succeed based on their own hard work, efforts, and merit.

5. *A Right is an Entitlement*

Progressives believe that certain groups are deserving of or entitled to certain privileges, and that it is government's role to provide these benefits. An example of this would be how the Occupy Wall Street crowd has demanded free college tuition and student debt relief.[xi] Certain groups believe that African Americans of today are entitled to "repayment" for the slavery of their ancestors more than 1 ½ centuries ago. The rights of citizenship and the ability to fulfill one's instincts in Capitalism are not the same as being "Entitled" to anything, whether it is a job, a pay scale, an education, abortions, or health care.

The belief that a person *deserves* a reward or benefit strips away the innate drive to achieve, and in turn degrades the sense of value people gain by working to provide for their well-being. Again, this cripples an individual's ability to rise up higher in Maslow's Pyramid.[xii] Opportunities make it possible for those in need to become self-reliant, not dependent on entitlements or redistribution of others' successes to get their needs met.

6. *Rationalizing Opposition To The Systems That Founded and Sustained The United States*

Many Progressives, (and a few Republican and Libertarian Isolationists), believe that Islamic terrorists exist due to foreign policy of the United States, and that military action only creates more anti-U.S. Muslims. Many also believe terrorism is a law enforcement problem and that terrorists should be tried in civilian, not military, courts. This approach to international relations and foreign policy goes back a long way. Think of Neville Chamberlain believing he could make "peace" with Hitler after Germany's invasion of Poland, Austria and other European countries.[xiii] After all, Chamberlain

21

believed Great Britain was not "Imperialist;" they were only great "traders" in their international reach, and were certainly not in conflict with Hitler over this…

Terrorism poses one of the greatest threats to our nation. The belief sets of radical Islam go back 1,500 years:

If you do not worship Allah as we do, you are an Infidel. Allah wants us to convert the entire world to Islam. It is fine for us to lie to Infidels if it serves this purpose of Allah. There are no innocents outside of Islam. Jihad is the holy war we fight with all Infidels, and to die in Jihad is a great blessing to you before Allah.

These are deeply rooted religious beliefs. How can you negotiate with a collection of people who view you as less than themselves, and lying to you only serves their God?

Irrespective of good or bad foreign policy, Progressives carry personal guilt that all suffering in the world is a result of the greed and self-interest of individuals and nations that become powerful. By this, they declare the instinctive nature of Capitalism as "evil" and the cause of all suffering. Apparently in their own minds, them coming to power is the only thing that can correct this evil - even if it means exonerating the outrageous beliefs of radical Islam.

7. *Key Elements of Survival - Including Health Care, Energy, and Wages to Laborers - Must Be Controlled by Government*

Whether it is "Green Energy Exploration" or government mandated health care, Progressives fundamentally believe it is government's responsibility to provide a baseline of survival and quality of life for all people. Most Progressives go beyond that and extend it to people who come to our country illegally, as "our greed and imperialism causes their suffering…"

This belief extends to Labor Unions which are "oppressed by business owners." (There are those greedy "capitalists" again.) It expands to education, as "everyone has a right to education so they can survive in the world," and beyond this to childcare, housing, transportation, and so on. Creeping control slowly and systematically takes over all freedom by feeding small doses of "sedative" to a growing population in any country. Like all addictions, the sedative doses grow until total addiction is achieved.

The Golden Rules of Economics in Progressives and Liberals

- The factual evidence of history, the state of today's world, and actual life experiences do not support the beliefs of Progressives and Liberals.
- Progressive and Liberal beliefs violate the basic human instinct of True Capitalism. By doing so, they rob and cheat both those from whom they are taking away personal rewards, and those to whom others' rewards are bequeathed.
- Progressives and Liberals believe they understand what individual people need and how to give it to them better than the individuals themselves.
- Like all tyrannies, Progressives and Liberals integrate their beliefs into the educational system and mainstream media to indoctrinate others into their beliefs.

6 THE GOLDEN RULES OF ECONOMICS IN POLITICAL POWER

Power is an interesting concept. If the curse on mankind in the Book of Genesis is true: *"By the sweat of your brow you shall eat bread 'til you return to the ground, for out of it you were taken; for dust you are, and to dust you shall return"* – then the simplest way out of the curse is to gain power and inflict the curse on someone else!

During the past 120 years, mankind has been able to set ourselves free from beliefs we carried for millennia. As a result, we have made great strides toward freeing ourselves from the labors described in the Book of Genesis. Better nutrition, health care, transportation, farming, communications, and housing have all benefited from setting free mankind's natural creative spirit.

Doing all this takes leadership, innovation, sacrifice and hard work. Most people believe that creator/producers should reap the rewards of their effort, but because of "power" that does not always take place. A great amount of power is probably the most seductive and addictive element of life that people face.

Why do people seek power? For some, it is to protect themselves from challenging and sometimes terrible life experiences. For others, it can be as simple as jealousy, or coveting what someone else has.

"(Getting) something for nothing, it never loses its charm." – Michael Lewis

There are many ways people can provide for themselves to ensure their own survival. Ideally people will work, innovate or create something of value, and become adequately good at trading for their efforts with others.

25

Those who discover they are not particularly inclined to invest the time, cost, and discipline to survive by these methods tend to gravitate toward either gaining power, or ingratiating themselves to the established power. After all, a position of power can be used to take from others whatever is needed or wanted.

Our Founding Fathers knew nobody is immune to delusions of power. They lived through the British trying to destroy the American colonies as economic competitors by crippling our free trade with the rest of the world. The British did this by forced shipping through their own import/export companies, and through excessive taxation on the colonies.

Our Founders' response was creating a government with built-in checks and balances (the three independent branches of government), and protection of each state's rights.

This system of government was not built on any type of false belief that Americans had higher ethical or moral values for their fellow citizens. It was built on the absolute knowledge that those citizens who engaged in governance would be deeply tempted by, and in many cases succumb to, corruptions of power. Our system of governance was thus built to:
1. Limit the amount of impact any single source of power could have on the country.
2. Provide regularly scheduled ways for the citizens of every state to replace those serving in their governments.

Despite these Constitutionally defined protections from abuse of power, the government has habitually created policies that increase its power and influence in our lives. There are old stories and new stories that expose this. For example, Congress and President Lincoln passed laws to expand railroads[xiv] through government subsidy that paid by the mile. *"Let's build them long, not build them by efficiency or quality."* Many of these railroad companies were owned both by politicians, (particularly Senators), and their cronies.

Today we call this "Washington Inc.," and it was this very practice in the late 18th Century by King George III that brought about the American Revolution.

There are always new stories of government increasing it's power and influence:

- 99 weeks of Unemployment Benefits.[xv]
- $530 million paid to Solyndra, **some of which was given to the California Democratic Party.**[xvi]
- The National Labor Relations Board blocking Boeing from building an aircraft assembly plant in South Carolina because South Carolina is a "right to work" state. This translates into businesses the size and type of Boeing being forced to hire only union laborers.[xvii]

The challenges go far beyond creating extremely unfair trading policies. For example, what happens when a business that is not viable on the free market gets government funds to substitute for profitability? Banks being "too big to fail" is a classic example of what this looks like.

Banks could not sustain their financial viability after the collapse of the housing market. Not to worry! The government will loan the banks money so they don't collapse, while at the same time increasing regulations that make it extremely difficult, if not impossible, for private businesses to borrow money. (Businesses often need borrowed money to stabilize, grow and hire new employees.)

What a dilemma. The bank is now "solvent" but prevented from engaging in business with the private sector in the U.S. economy. Not to worry! The government could not afford to bail out the banks, so the government has to borrow money to pay for the bailout. From whom does the government borrow this money? They borrow from the now "solvent" banks of course, with sufficient interest payments for the banks to turn a profit.

This type of unfair trading practice actually violates a core nature in people – the instinctive drive to participate in fair trade with others in order to enhance our ability to provide for ourselves. The trades are no longer fair. Average citizens cannot compete with a government controlled by Progressives, Liberals, Democrats and "ruling class" inside-the-beltway Republicans. Without everyone realizing it, we are all being cheated.

This innate drive to freely barter and trade goods has been a part of human civilization throughout history. Even young children delight in trading with one another – giving up something of value to get something in return. No one has to teach this to them; they come to it naturally!

When people become aware that their means of survival and provision are being compromised, they normally would react aggressively.

How does government avoid open rebellion from those they wronged in their own society?

For at least 60 years the Progressive/Liberal leaders of our government have continually created policies that violate fair trade, thus threatening people's instinctive drive to trade for survival.

Progressive/Liberal leadership has, up to this point, avoided triggering an outright rebellion by telling people they have a *right* to certain things.

Simply put, government policy and programs provide things that people are led to believe they are "owed." Mainstream media and our educational system are just as much to blame in establishing and perpetuating these lies. By this, the entitled citizens are pacified, and rather than rebel against the personal destruction that their government is creating, sufficient numbers of them become dependent on government providing for them.

Historically it is a new idea that society is owed social benefits and that government's purpose is to satisfy human needs. This is a central idea in Marxism, developed in the 19th Century.[xviii]

The truth is individuals have a right to the opportunity to engage in free and fair trade to provide for themselves and their families. It is the government's responsibility to protect this opportunity for all of its citizens. When the government's policies extend into manipulating trade practices it becomes an abuse of the power that has been granted to them by the Constitution. Worse than that, it is a violation of the innate instinct that compels people into fair trade practices.

The preamble to our Constitution states that one of the purposes of the American government is to "*promote* the general welfare." To promote means to support or foster. Supporting and fostering the general welfare implies making a way for the needs of the people to be met. This is not the same as *providing* for the general welfare.

Now we come to the hub of the issue. The seduction of power has placed people in our government, both in elected officials and employees (lifetime bureaucrats), who will sacrifice anything to maintain their power, and by that their own Money and their Safety, all at the expense of our citizens.

The Golden Rules of Economics in Political Power
- Despite the best efforts of our Founding Fathers, the Constitution, and Bill of Rights, the seduction of power has corrupted the governance of our country.
- Politicians' and bureaucrats' addiction to money, safety, and government power is leading to the economic collapse of the United States.

THE GOLDEN RULES OF ECONOMICS

7 THE GOLDEN RULES OF ECONOMICS IN BUREAUCRATS

Few people in the private sector understand the lives of those in public sector employment. Let's look at the circumstances of federal employees' jobs.

Benefits for Federal Employees

Vacation
- 10 paid holidays per year
- 13 paid vacation days for 1-3 years' service
- 20 paid vacation days for 3-15 years' service
- 26 paid vacation days for 15+ years' service
- Military service counts and is an automatic 26 days

Sick leave
13 paid sick days per year[xix]

Think of it! Three years of federal employment and you get 43 days of vacation and sick leave per year. Time that right on the weekends and you can add four more days based on when national holidays fall. If you reach 15 years of employment, you get 49 days off per year; almost two whole months!

Flexibilities
- Flexible work schedules
- Telework (access to working remotely)
- Programs for child care and elder care
- Subsidies and dependent care flexible spending accounts
- Employee assistance programs[xx]

Retirement Plans
- 401K plans matched up to 5% of employees' contributions[xxi]

Health benefits

- The government's health benefits program has about 350 health care plan options throughout the United States. There are at least a dozen available to each employee.[xxii]
- Dental[xxiii] and vision[xxiv] coverage is also available to employees, retirees and eligible family members
- Flexible Spending Accounts are also available[xxv]

Miscellaneous

- Pay incentives for relocation, retention and recruitment for certain positions[xxvi]
- Special consideration for student loan repayment[xxvii]
- Postal workers pay considerably less for their health benefits than competitive federal civil service employees, due to negotiated contracts[xxviii]

How many private sector jobs offer these kinds of options?

Salaries

Federal workers have been awarded bigger average pay and benefit increases than private employees for nine years in a row. The compensation gap between federal and private workers has doubled in the past decade.

Federal civil servants earned average pay and benefits of $123,049 in 2009 while private workers made $61,051 in total compensation, according to the Bureau of Economic Analysis.

The federal compensation advantage has grown from $30,415 in 2000 to $61,998 in 2009.

Public employee unions say the compensation gap reflects the increasingly high levels of skill and education required for most federal jobs, and government contracting lower-paid jobs to the private sector in recent years.

This is according to the Bureau of Economic Analysis and an article by Dennis Cauchon of *USA Today* on August 13, 2010.[xxix]

Termination of Federal Employees

The federal government is pretty mysterious on finding grounds for firing an employee. We were able to gather these pieces of information:

Federal government employees may have greater job protection than most private sector employees, but that does not mean they are completely secure. There are situations when federal agencies may legally terminate the employment of a federal employee. Those situations differ according to the federal agency and type of employee involved.

Termination of Career Employees

There are primarily two legal ways federal agencies may terminate a career employee. First, an agency may be forced to downsize its workforce for reasons unrelated to a specific employee's job performance, such as a budget reduction, decreased workload, or shifting national priorities. If an agency is forced to downsize, it must consider these four factors when making layoffs:

1. Type of employment (career employee, appointee, or probationary employee for example)
2. Length of government service
3. Veteran's preference rights
4. Performance ratings

To fire an employee over poor performance, substandard performance must be properly documented in formal performance reviews. Employees must be provided with the opportunity to correct their behavior. If an employee does not make the correction, then an agency may follow procedures to terminate employment. Those procedures include providing written notice to the employee.[xxx]

Termination of Probationary or Appointed Employees

Probationary employees and government appointees have fewer rights than federal government career employees. Probationary employees are technically still job applicants, despite receiving a paycheck. Appointees serve at the pleasure of the President or for a certain term, and thus do not have a reasonable expectation of a lifelong career in their current position. That said, while their positions may be terminated, they cannot be fired for discriminatory reasons or for exercising their legally protected rights. Employees of certain intelligence or defense agencies may also have fewer protections against job terminations than civilian career employees.[xxxi]

<u>Sources:</u>
United States Office of Personnel Management
www.usajobs.gov

Bureau of Economic Analysis
Dennis Cauchon – *USA Today* 8/13/2010

Merit Systems Protection Board
www.MSPB.org

The saddest part of the government labor force is there are very limited incentives for increasing productivity, reducing budgets, being competitive with the private sector, or becoming efficient. Rather, the security of the position results in a comfortable lifestyle with little motivation or reward for improving. After all, government employees do not engage in the instinctive Capitalism all people in the private sector must follow.

Even Franklin Delano Roosevelt understood this when he stated that federal employees should not be unionized. FDR said, "*The prospect of a strike by a government union is unthinkable and intolerable.*" He knew there was no leverage against federal employee unions negotiating with the government. Forcing the government by contract to only employ union workers creates an atrocious situation: Government services, and the citizens they employ, are a monopoly. Monopolies have no concern about competitiveness, efficiency or even "keeping it honest."

In 1989 I was visiting an assistant secretary of George Herbert Walker Bush's cabinet in Washington, DC. To avoid any negative impact, I will leave out the name of the agency.

The assistant secretary was very conscientious to follow all federal rules. I couldn't take him out to lunch, or even buy him a cup of coffee. We met in the agency's cafeteria, and he told me he was retiring in three months after 40 years of service in the agency. I was fascinated; he had been there since 1949. I asked if he minded answering this question:

"*You have served under nine Presidents: Harry Truman, Dwight D. Eisenhower, Jack Kennedy, Lyndon Baines Johnson, Richard Nixon, Gerald Ford, Jimmy Carter, Ronald Reagan, and now George H. W. Bush. Who was the best to serve under?*"

34

The assistant secretary never hesitated, and his answer stunned me. *"That is an easy question. All those guys, every one of them, came into office thinking they were going to do "this" to improve the Agency, or "that" to shift the impact of the Agency, but Richard Nixon, he knew. Richard Nixon knew that he would only be there 4 years or 8 years, and both long before he got here and long after he left, I would still be here, so he left us alone..."*

So what do we have today? Rapidly growing, overpaid, unionized, public employees in many agencies producing substandard results seems to be the norm rather than the exception.

The Golden Rules of Economics in Bureaucrats
- Bureaucrats, by nature of their jobs, are not driven by efficiency or profitability.
- Bureaucrats are driven by a desire to keep their jobs, increase their income, and increase their retirement pensions.
- Bureaucrats can only be managed by strict budgets that do not bankrupt the U.S. economy.

THE GOLDEN RULES OF ECONOMICS

8 THE GOLDEN RULES OF ECONOMICS IN FEDERAL BUDGETS

In 1963 Lyndon B. Johnson, known for his domineering personality and coercion of powerful politicians, took over as president after John F. Kennedy's assassination. The event left the nation in mourning and shock, and was permanently burned in the memories of all who were alive at the time. This tragedy set the stage for LBJ to drive through many programs rejected by Congress in JFK's "New Frontier" as the programs became politically feasible under a new label.

LBJ took advantage of the crisis and created a handful of government programs under the label of the "Great Society." These programs included federal aid to education, and creation of Medicare, Medicaid, Urban Renewal, Head Start, Food Stamps and others. [xxxii]

As you can imagine, all these programs cost a lot of money. Federal education aid, for example, rose 270% during LBJ's six-year term.[xxxiii] Medicare started as a low cost program near $100 million in federal expenditures and quickly jumped 56 times its original price tag.[xxxiv] These large programs, along with an unpopular and costly war in Vietnam, left the government in need of money.

The typical working Americans scraping by, but not on these programs, were trapped in a dilemma. Previously they had the choice to provide voluntarily for the needy or elderly from what they earned. They made this choice based on what they believed was fair and what they could afford. The new programs caused them, as the non-poverty taxpayers, to foot the bills. Regular people moved from free will to involuntary payment. This was true as the programs rose in cost each year or continued forever, regardless of whether or not they agreed with the programs' actions.

As you can imagine, this didn't go over well with all Americans. In 1969, Richard Nixon became president. At first he escalated the Vietnam War and continued the spending binge, for example creating the Environmental Protection Agency (EPA).[xxxv]

But as every household instinctively knows, you can only spend at high rates so long before having to pay the piper. Nixon's time was up; he had to do something to appease the people. Americans were getting frustrated with putting the huge spending on the government's credit card each year. This led up to the Congressional Budget and Impoundment Control Act of 1974, which created the Congressional Budget Office (CBO).[xxxvi]

The CBO is supposed to provide Congress with objective analysis to aid budgetary decisions.[xxxvii] Most importantly, they establish baseline budgets. The baselines are designed to show what would happen if current budgetary policies continued in the future.

Think of a line graph where the line always rises over time. This is the baseline. The reason the line (or projection) is always rising is certain programs have automatic increases built in to them.[xxxviii] Each program has different automatic increase rates.

The automatic increases have been established from many congressional revisions. For example, a new Act in 1985 decided the rate by which Social Security and Unemployment Insurance would increase each year automatically.[xxxix] These increases take place *without* Congressional approval each year. They are automatic.

It would be really similar to you deciding that your household budget for travel will go up by 8% each year no matter if your income goes up or down.

That kind of irresponsible behavior isn't the worst. The worst is how those in power tell the public what is happening regarding spending and budget cuts.

Let's go back to President Nixon at a time when citizens were growing tired of the high spending. Upon creating the CBO, Nixon and other members of the political elite were able to tell the people they are cutting budgets, when budgets were steadily and relentlessly rising over time.

How did they do this? Simple: Smoke and mirrors.

As an example, what if you plan to automatically increase your travel budget each year by 8% and you only spend 6% more. According to how the CBO calculates things that means you saved 2%.[xl] It doesn't matter that you increased your budget an additional 6% more than last year. In their language, you "SAVED" 2%.

This kind of budget gimmickry done by officers in a private corporation would land those officers in prison. This type of budget gimmickry done in Washington appeases voters by drowning out the real story in catchy headlines (e.g., Spending to be Cut $1 Trillion) and thus secures those politicians' future positions in power.

In reality, what does this mean? The financial services industry has a mathematical guideline they use in helping their clients build wealth. It is called "The Rule of 72." What this rule means is if you take the "average" percentage rate of growth and divide it into 72, that number represents the number of years before your initial investment doubles. In other words, if you invested $1 million and it had an annual rate of return of 8% it would double to $2 million in nine years (72/8 = 9).

That means that every decade, the actual federal budget DOUBLES without additional programs (such as health care) added by Congress and the President. This figure does not include additional costs to business of increased regulatory laws.

Federal taxes ultimately are tied to how large the nation's total spending is. This is called the Gross Domestic Product (GDP). Historically, if the GDP grows at certain annual percentages (typically 4% to 6%) the economy is healthy. If it grows at too slow a rate (3% or less), the country is in a recession or depression. If it grows too fast we are in an inflation, where goods' and services' costs go up faster than income.

Did you notice the "guarantee of failure"? If the economy grows at a healthy rate (4% to 6%), that growth cannot keep up with the automatic 8% growth in the federal government, even if there is no additional spending by Congress. Heaven help us if the economy only grows at the rate it has in the from 2009 through 2012 (1% to 3%).

Tragically, both parties have practiced this kind of behavior. It has gone unnoticed. As American citizens, we have had the rug pulled out from under us.

The Golden Rules of Economics in Federal Budgets

- Automatic budget increases have created an uncontrolled financial crisis in the United States.
- You cannot increase spending on federal budgets faster than the growth of the GDP without terrible consequences.
- Government employees are not driven to efficiency or profitability. They are driven to security and pensions. Without control of their budgets, the private sector will fail at paying for the federal budget.
- The U.S. economy fails unless Congress removes automatic spending increases.

9 THE GOLDEN RULES OF ECONOMICS IN BANKING

Few people clearly understand how banks work. Like any other business, they have a product; theirs is money. Money is the way we all determine the value of trades, and trades are the basis for not only our survival, but also how well we create the lifestyles and communities we desire. How banks trade their product makes the difference between creation of a new factory or using their product to pay the federal government's debt.

Thousands of individual bankers stationed in every city in America have acted for generations as gatekeepers for deciding where their product winds up. Since the early 1990s through the economic crisis in 2008, right up to today, the federal government has increasingly taken on a controlling role of being the gatekeeper of money. Banks have been forced to operate how the federal government wants them to, and government control has grown outrageously larger because of the federal government's debt; when you spend more than you have, you must borrow the money from somewhere. Our government borrows a large portion of it from our banks.

Most people know the story of Rumpelstiltskin who could turn straw into gold. I've often wondered if you could really do this. While I have not been able to find little trolls in the forest who could pull this off, I did find something the Federal Reserve Board and banks do each month that comes pretty close.

The United States budget is currently around $3.82 trillion. Collected taxes account for $2.17 trillion of this amount. The rest, $1.65 trillion, is a shortfall and has to be borrowed to cover expenses.[xli] The Government (meaning we taxpayers) borrows 60% of this $1.65 trillion from banks each year, while 40% is borrowed from foreign countries.

How do we borrow the 60% from ourselves to pay ourselves?

The Federal Reserve and United States Treasury sell our debt. They do this each month at an event called the Treasury Auction. Our debt is sold in the form of bonds; think U.S. Savings Bonds but on a giant scale.[xlii] In the early stages of the auction only certain banks and countries can buy these bonds because the amounts are so large. In a typical month the Fed and Treasury can sell $113 billion of bonds.

The largest foreign holder of our debt is China, which buys and holds roughly 8% of our debt each month. The Government (YOU) on the other hand buys 60% each month.

Let me say that again. YOU buy $67 billion of your own debt each month.

To do this, the government has to make money out of thin air! In simple terms, this is how it is done:
1. The Federal Reserve asks the Treasury to sell $113 Billion in bonds (our monthly shortfall). The Fed knows they can sell 40% of the bonds each month to China and other foreign markets.
2. The Fed then goes to a select group of banks (think Morgan Stanley) called Primary Dealers and asks them to buy the other 60% by **lending** them the money to do it.
3. The dealers take the money from the Fed as a short-term loan with a low interest rate and they purchase the bonds.
4. The Treasury now has $67 billion it can spend and is left with a bond it has to pay back to the bondholders over time at a low fixed interest rate.

So far it sounds pretty good. All sane nations of the world do this to raise money. Think of it as taking a loan against your credit card. As long as you generate excess money (cash) each month to pay the card back, this is not a problem.

But the money to pay back *our card* comes out of the $3.82 trillion budget.

We have not generated excess cash (taxes) out of our economy for years. When we have, it has not gone to pay down the debt, but has been spent by Congress. *This* is why we have to borrow (**$1.65 trillion**) in the first place!

Over time, the amount you have to borrow to pay back what you owe gets bigger. That means the amount you have to make out of thin air gets bigger.

Finally you end up with an amount owed you can never pay back. Think Greece right now.

Back to the banks:
1. China and other countries that buy our bonds use excess capital (their positive tax revenue and other income) to purchase them in most cases.
2. We use debt to buy our debt.
3. The banks in turn collect a small transaction fee for helping the Fed.
4. This fee covers the cost of borrowing the money and buying the bonds.
5. This is a massive moneymaker for the Primary Dealers. Even a 1% transaction fee on $67 billion is $670 million. *That is each month.*

If we were to have a failed bond auction it would portray a lack of confidence in our country to the world. The 40% of our bonds bought by the rest of the world would be at risk.

This would call into question our status as a global leader, so each month, no matter how much in bonds comes up for sale, the *Primary Dealers make sure to buy them all.*

Up until 2011 it was rare for any country to have a failed Bond Auction. Today, Europe is having them daily due to worries over their debt levels.[xliii]

It gets better:
• The Primary Dealers can then sell the bonds in smaller amounts in the secondary market to hedge funds, pensions, 401k plans and anyone else who wants them – for a small fee of course.
• The Primary Dealers then give back the original amount to the Fed and the Fed is set to do it the next month all over again.

This is how you end up holding your own debt. Like I said, sounds pretty good so far. There is one problem though – the government owes the bondholder an interest payment as well as a principal payment at the end of the bond's maturity date.

As of June of 2012 our debt on these bonds has passed *$15,000,000,000,000.00* (**$15 trillion**).

We (the taxpayers) owe ourselves $10.3 trillion and foreign governments are owed $4.7 trillion.

During the time when President Obama and the Democratic-Party controlled Congress had been in office our debt has gone up by **$4.4 trillion**.[xliv] This amount does not take into account the costs of the health care bill, jobs program, or anything else we spend money on.

Governments have always used this bank trick to sell debt. That in itself is not the real problem. The true problem is the 8% annual federal budget increases and the continuing out-of-control spending on new programs that force us to absorb larger and larger debt payments year after year.

It puts us at a disadvantage internationally as we have to "be nice to those countries" that buy our debt. It takes away our spending power and ability to grow our economy.

Interest rates in the U.S. have to be kept low, not to help the economy, but to keep our interest payments on bonds low. In Europe, for some countries, a 1% increase in interest rates amounts to $38 billion in extra payments per year.

At current debt loads a **1% increase** in the U.S. would mean **$150 billion in extra interest payments each year.**

This has to stop. If we continue at our current rate of spending, all our taxes will go to debt servicing. This is not fixable by simply raising taxes on the rich.

Even if you taxed 100% of the income from the wealthiest 1% of citizens you would only cover the debt shortfall for seven months.[xlv]

The effect is far worse, as the 1% would have no money to spend; the taxes generated by their money being circulated through the economy (the velocity of money) would be gone. Actual total tax collection would drop significantly.

The next year you would still be $1.65 trillion short and would have no way to solve the debt problem outside of taking it from the 99%.

The net-net result? Banks had no money to loan after the collapse of the housing market. The federal government rescued them with a "too big to fail" policy of lending them money the Fed did not have, and then borrowing it back from the banks to pay for the loan.

The Golden Rules of Economics in Banking

- The federal government is spending far more money than it has.
- The federal government makes up the money they need by borrowing it from the banks in the form of selling bonds to the banks.
- Banks do not have enough money to lend to the federal government, so the Federal Reserve prints money (they increase the M1 – the money supply) in order to loan money to the banks.
- Also the profits for the banks from the interest payments on the bonds give the banks money to buy the government bonds.
- The federal government has now "back doored" a way for banks to have money to "lend" to the government.
- The federal government is killing the U.S. economy by absorbing almost all the lending capacity of banks away from the private sector.

10 BREAKING THE GOLDEN RULES OF ECONOMICS IN PEOPLE

When you enter into a contest where your opponent has not only made up the rules, but changes them to their own liking as you play, even an "act of God" will not let you "win." Progressives, Liberals, and the Democratic Party have been defining the rules for years, and the Republican Party has either been complicit, naïve, or just plain stupid in playing by their rules.

When current commentators, talk show hosts, politicians and candidates try to debate the issues, they always wind up playing by rules the enemy set up. Frankly, many politicians and candidates don't understand that their opponents ARE an enemy. President Barak Obama was the embodiment of all the policies of Progressives, Liberals, and European style Socialists over the past 60 years. The saddest part of all is the President, along with many others in his political party, actually *believe* their policies work despite no historical or "real-time" evidence. They are unwilling and unable to change, even in the face of the truth.

To halt this certain economic destruction of our nation we must redefine the Rules of the Game. I believe this book does just that. Every policy challenge, every economic issue, every class warfare tactic can be destroyed by clearly understanding the real Golden Rules of Economics. I hope you will join the many citizens who are taking an aggressive, long term stand against the insanities that our Founding Fathers revolted against. This time it will be a quiet revolution, won at the ballot box over many election cycles.

I trust you will enjoy this and the following chapters where we lay out policy-by-policy, topic-by-topic, how The Golden Rules of Economics have been violated, and how you have cleverly been cheated in the trades that define your lives...[xlvi]

Perhaps the easiest way to understand how these Golden Rules are violated is based on understanding differences of childhood and adulthood.

At some point in their lives most people who get married want to raise a family. Families who love and support each other are the most marvelous experience in life. Families that somehow break down can become the most painful and vicious experience in living. As are most things in life, what you do with what you are given makes all the difference in the world as to what you experience.

Most of us know the experience of people having a baby:
"She's so beautiful…"
"He's going to be an athlete…"
"He has his father's hair and his mother's brains…"
"She has her grandmother's personality…"

Babies can be the most rewarding, encouraging, exhausting, expensive, and sleep depriving experience of someone's life up to that time. Yet, in most cases, we truly love them.

Babies and young children are wholly dependent. They cannot provide the food they need to eat, the clothes they need to wear, or the shelter they require to stay physically safe. They cannot educate themselves, learn to get along socially, or leave their personal selfishness without instruction, teaching, patience, rewards, or discipline.

The measure of sacrifice necessary to raise a child is unfathomable to anyone who has not attempted to do it. What does the child give you in return?
"I love you mom…"
"Dad, I had fun shopping with you today…"
"Mom, can my friends come over to play?"
"I'm scared. Will you hold me?"

As children grow, they go through many challenges. These range from massive biophysical changes through puberty, to puppy love, to being betrayed by a "best friend forever," to forming opinions about an unbelievable number of topics. Their beliefs begin to be formed, and their willingness to talk about them can grow to unfettered proportions. At a certain point they rebel against their mother and father. At another point they sense a need to "break away from home."

All these are normal parts of growing up. They are all very challenging, both for children and their parents.

For a very few children in today's world, they must find jobs to help support themselves and their families, or because it is a discipline their parents insist they learn. For most of the rest, they are sheltered, protected, and provided for throughout their entire childhood, and for many this continues throughout their years in college.

There are many objectives to raising a child. These might include:
- Discovering who they are and building self confidence
- Growing in character and basic moral principles
- Finding out what your child loves to do, and making a way for them to do it
- Hoping they find the right person to spend the rest of their life with
- Keeping your relationship solid with your children for a lifetime
- Giving them life skills – can they wash their clothes or boil an egg?

A critical part of raising a child is to prepare them for adulthood. What requirements of adulthood are different from childhood? At a minimum these include:
- How to survive in a world that is not always fair
- How to create a "safe" set of relationships that will be with them throughout their lives
- How to deal with the world wisely
- How to earn a living so they can provide for themselves

I grew up in an immigrant family. My father's family in the "Old Country" (Greece) was an educated, successful group that was economically destroyed by Nazi occupation during World War II. My father, the oldest son, came here to help support his two brothers' educations. One became a noted heart surgeon. The other became the Fleet Captain of the second largest oil tanker line in the world. The family recovered until the consequences of Greek Socialism began to take its toll in the 1980s. I understood that I went to college to create a career. I did not go to college because "everyone has to" or because "it is the next thing to do."

Unfortunately, that is not the case today.

In April 2011, students at the University of California-Merced were asked if they would be willing to sign a petition allowing redistribution of their GPAs to students having trouble fulfilling graduation requirements. Those students with an "excessive" GPA of 4.0 would have a reduction to 3.8 GPA and the extra 0.2 points given to a less privileged student unable to satisfy the school's academic requirements.[xlvii]

Similar questions were asked to students at DePaul University in Chicago, Illinois in October 2009, only this time the proposal was to support the Academic Redistribution and Reinvestment Act.[xlviii] This proposal would allow students with a GPA of 4.0 to be assessed 30%, and then 1.2 points of their GPA would be added to the general academic bank account and re-distributed to all students with a 2.0 GPA or lower. The GPA of all students would then average out to approximately 2.7 and all would be able to graduate. This is only fair, right?

How did students in both examples respond when asked what they thought of these proposals? One student responded by saying, "*Why do I have to sacrifice my grade-point average if I am doing my work?*" Another student said, "*This isn't fair, I work for what I have!*"

In contrast, when these students were asked about taxing the top wage earners in the country to redistribute that wealth to the poor, they agreed this was fair. They have a personal connection to their own hard-earned GPAs, but identifying with the category of wage earners who have a portion of their wealth redistributed was a different story. It's a lot easier to distribute what isn't yours!

These students never learned a critical lesson of becoming an adult:

You are responsible for your own survival and provision.

They were sheltered and protected by their parents (and in today's world, by the Progressive policies of the federal government). It kept them from learning that they must support themselves. This thought never occurred to this collection of college students.

Either their parents never taught them, or they refused to learn. It is a certainty they were not taught it in the educational systems they experienced.

In 2009, the polling firm Ayers-McHenry asked respondents to choose the statement about government policies that came closest to their views:

"Government policies should promote fairness by narrowing the gap between rich and poor, spreading the wealth, and making sure that economic outcomes are more equal;" or *"Government policies should promote opportunity by fostering job growth, encouraging entrepreneurs, and allowing people to keep more of what they earn."*

The second statement, *"Government policies should promote opportunity..."* was chosen by 63% over the first option. Government promoting *"fairness"* was chosen by only 31% of polling respondents.[xlix]

Today's young adults wind up coming into the world not knowing The Golden Rules. Far worse, they believe it is their right to violate all of these rules, as long as it is to their own benefit or the benefit of those they believe are "worthy."

Bottom Line? We all pay for their lack of never leaving childhood.

Take this a few steps further – what does total dependency on Welfare or Food Stamps bring about? How far out should unemployment benefits run? At what point does dependency destroy the "adult" premises of life?

How about ironclad union contracts that lack clauses to promote efficiency or profit-sharing based on specific guidelines of a company's profitability? Are workers in this environment motivated to produce more, or are they singled out for "the consequences of making their fellow workers look bad"?

Are we facing the same issue with teachers' unions in public schools? How about government employees? Is there any incentive to become efficient, increase contributions, or stay within budgets? There certainly are no "profit" incentives, as neither entity is anything more than a dependent service to the community and nation.

The sadness of this story goes on and on. Many people working in those organizations either never "reached" adulthood, or are penalized for working effectively as an adult. Eventually, without controls, these organizations kill the systems that provide them their incomes.

There is a difference between the private sector (profit-driven organizations in the economy) and the public sector (government agencies, public schools, and national organizations such as labor unions and education). The private sector is driven to improve efficiency, profitability and the overall prosperity of the nation; they instinctively know that rising prosperity for everyone increases their own prosperity.

Many public sectors never learn this. They are not driven to increase the overall prosperity of the nation. They are driven to increase their personal stability, income, retirement, and ultimately, lack of responsibility for their performance.

Progressives and many economists believe that the money placed into the economy by the public sector is just as valuable as the money placed into the economy by the private sector. There is nothing further from the truth.

The private sector wants economic activity to increase pace in a safe way. That function is called "The Velocity of Money." The faster the Velocity of Money, the more transactions take place. The more transactions take place, the more economic activity occurs, and, the more taxes get collected.

The public sector has no motivation or need to increase the Velocity of Money. In fact, the public sector works against building efficiency. Greater efficiency means smaller budgets and lower benefits to them.

The economy can never recover by trying to increase its activity through the public sector, regardless of what economists, the President, Progressives, Liberals, Democrats, or certain collections of Republicans tell you. In fact, it has just the opposite effect:
1. It slows down the private sector.
2. That slows down the Velocity of Money.
3. That reduces taxes.
4. That creates deficit spending on programs with automatic budget increases.
5. That creates a larger federal deficit with every new program that is enacted.
6. That further slows down the private sector.
7. That, and more … you get the idea.

We have reached the point where the government and leaders in the public sectors MUST learn the true hard lessons of life.

They have to stop being children.

They must become adults.

More importantly, American citizens must learn that childhood behaviors in adults are robbing and cheating all of us.

Unless their activities, policies, and programs are reversed, and rapidly, we may never recover from their childlike follies.

The Golden Rules of Economics in People
- Each person must make a contribution to his/her community that is regarded as having value in order to provide for their own basic needs (Safety).
- People are only owed the right to pursue opportunities that may come along. They do not have the right to "demand" an opportunity, only the *right* to pursue opportunities without bias or prejudice.
- People have the right to engage in "trade" with others if they so choose.
- It is the responsibility of parents and schools to educate children in these Truths.
- It is the responsibility of communities and government to protect people's right to pursue opportunity.
- There is NO guarantee any opportunity pursued will be fulfilled.

Don't you feel cheated in the trade? You should – it is about to destroy the America our forefathers created for our joint benefit...

11 BREAKING THE GOLDEN RULES OF ECONOMICS IN CAPITALISM

Chapter 3 spent time blowing away smoke from the true definition of Capitalism. The magnitude of examples of how The Golden Rules of Capitalism are being violated by the federal government could fill an encyclopedia, but it is worthwhile to spend some time in this chapter giving a few clear examples. Until a dominant majority of voting American citizens understands this, we will never free ourselves from the crippling effect of our government breaking The Golden Rules and cheating us in the trade.

Going Back To Our True History

The Founding Fathers structured our Federal Government on the premise that power and money would indeed corrupt its members, and because of that they devised elegant checks and balances to safeguard against horrible effects of government that destroy fundamental, inalienable rights of mankind. Mostly, they created an election process in which citizens could replace bad leadership with (hopefully) better leadership at least every two years.

The basic cause of the American Revolution was that British shippers and import/export companies could not economically compete with their counterparts in the original 13 States. As American entrepreneurs grew in size and global impact, Great Britain began to suffer economically, both at the import/export level (the basis for the financial survival of the global Great Britain), and governmental level (there was less money for King George and the Parliament).

In most cases of free market competition, all companies either find ways to improve their efficiency and performance, or they wind up with a smaller market share, possibly even shutting down. In the Great Britain of that time, the concept of economic efficiency and performance were ideas that went against the grain of how government and big business worked.

Great Britain had many colonies (Australia, Canada, New Zealand, the American Colonies, South Africa, and so on…) captured by British navies and armies, populated by British citizens who perhaps were not the "best fit" for England. These colonies became part of a "feeder system" of raw materials, goods and services to build the empire and provide economic advantage to England and the Crown.

This took place by the King and Parliament providing advantages to shipping and import/export companies that, in one way or another, "paid" for the privilege of exclusivity or limited competition in their "routes." Unfortunately for them, the upstart Americans refused to "abide" in these sets of rules, and engaged in what they believed were fair trades for their efforts.

As this began to take its toll on the King and Parliament's money coffers, Great Britain did not respond kindly. American shipping vessels were labeled pirates, and boarded and ransacked by British naval ships if caught. Finally, the ultimate indignation occurred when the King proclaimed excessive taxes on goods imported to the American colonies. This resulted in the Tea Party in Boston Harbor, and the American Revolution began. *"Taxation without Representation"* was the charge against King George, and a bitter war ensued.

Congress (both the House and the Senate), the administration (the Presidency and the agencies that make up the Cabinet), and the Judiciary (the interpretation of the Constitution, and federal laws and statutes), were structured to avoid how Great Britain tried to ransack the American Colonies economically.

It is very important to understand that "mercantilism" is not Capitalism. The definition of Capitalism is *"an economic system of barter (trade), in which all trading partners believe they receive equal or greater value in exchange for what they give up."* Mercantilism makes no pretense of *all* trading partners receiving equal value. By its intrinsic purpose, Mercantilism is designed to give unequal advantage to the business that receives the advantages of the Government's regulations or laws while providing unending power and privilege to people in government.

This form of economics has been around since the Dark Ages. In Europe this took on an economic form we know as Feudalism. The American

56

Revolution broke a system that oppressed its citizens for nearly two thousand years.

The "Ruling Class" does not want to give up its advantages. Self-interest prevails, along with safety, provision, protection, and all the elements Maslow's Theory says people need. Unfortunately, the appetite of the Ruling Class has grown so voracious there is not enough money available to feed its demands.

Today there are politicians, both Democrat and Republican, who make up this Ruling Class. There are many individuals in large business, in banking, finance, securities, manufacturing, and other sectors who make up this Ruling Class. There are individuals in Labor Unions who make up this Ruling Class. There are individuals in higher education and national defense who make up this Ruling Class. There are individuals in "Mainstream Media" who make up this Ruling Class.

This is the true definition of insider politics. The Ruling Class works "inside" politics to maintain power and money. This system is a UFO attack: They are Undermining Fair Opportunity.

It is a curious economic system. In a sense it is that word again, *Kleptonomics* – where *Klepto* in Greek means "to steal." It is an economic system designed to steal from those who are not part of the Ruling Class.

The key to the Ruling Class staying in power is them doing what they believe is necessary to avoid another revolution. Another economic revolution will result in them being thrown out of power, and by that, losing absolute control of the money.

Those voted into political office run our nation, therefore the key to sustaining Kleptonomics is to keep getting voted into office. How this has been done the past 50 years is a longer book than this, but what are the basics of what has been done?

First, **Ignore the true definition of Capitalism.** In Ruling Class language define Capitalism with talking points such as "the rich get richer," "the rich do not pay their fair share," "Capitalism just takes advantage of the working class," and so on.

Second, **Tie the abuses of business that are part of the Ruling Class into the definition of Capitalism**: "Of course it is unfair… look at what (name your current big company target) has done!"

What has been done? The Ruling Class plays insider politics to undermine real Capitalism. We are immersed in an economic system of unfair trades - actual thievery. This is the true definition of today's Washington government.

Do we have examples of this today? I am tempted to say, "Does the Pope live in Rome?" Let's look at some simple examples.

Inside the Unfair Advantage
In a recent report by CBS News *60 Minutes*, an investigation found that members of Congress and their aides have regular access to powerful political insider intelligence, and many have made well-timed stock market trades in the various industries they regulate.[1]

In simpler terms, this looks a lot like asking defendants to also be jurors at their own trial – a situation that could only happen in Washington.

Another example is the recent scandal of Solyndra's bankruptcy after government loans were granted. This occurred when the administration knew they were negative on the books for quite some time.[li] Some of these loans became significant contributions to the Democratic Party of California.[lii]

Also uncovered were a long list of energy loans made to President Obama's top fundraisers and supporters. The list reveals 80 percent of all $20.5 billion in Department of Energy loans went to Obama's top donors.[liii]

As some might remember, President Obama, when first proposing the Government Assistance (or bailout) plan, stated this process would be nonpartisan and fair. In fact, let President Obama's words speak for him:

"Decisions about how Recovery money will be spent will be based on the merits. They will not be made as a way of doing favors for lobbyists," Obama said in 2009.[liv]

The book titled *Throw Them All Out* by author Peter Schweizer exposes the insider trading and unfair advantages Congressmen and women have in stock trades and "get rich quick" maneuvers. [lv]

Breaking The Golden Rules of Capitalism shows from the years of *"do as I say not as I do"* that still covers Washington today.

Most of us believe that Americans vote in our leaders to do what's best for the country, businesses, communities, and families. Washington's elected officials are there for the public good, not for their own private gain.

If you were to have access like Congress does and take action on insider stock trades, you can bet the Securities and Exchange Commission (SEC) would surely prosecute you. You would go to jail. The hypocrisy is clear – if private individuals can be jailed or fined for trading on insider information, then our lawmakers should also be required to live by the same standards.

Is there any rationale for this behavior?

A new study from the Kellogg School of Management labeled *Power Increases Hypocrisy* explores why powerful people – many of whom intend to take a moral high ground – end up **not** practicing what they preach. [lvi] The research found that power makes people stricter in moral judgment of others, while going easier on themselves. In other words, they are seduced by the power they are given.

The level of Washington's hypocrisy and insider politics has never been on display so vividly as it is today. Double standard behaviors have been allowed for so long that Washington has been left out of touch with reality. We must stop turning our heads in ignorance.

So: Do you feel cheated in the Trade?

12 BREAKING THE GOLDEN RULES OF ECONOMICS IN WASHINGTON INC.

Why did the $800 billion in TARP (Troubled Asset Relief Program) money not create an economic recovery? Surely, pouring that much new spending into the Gross Domestic Product should have lit up at least some portions of commerce in the United States.

Is there a difference between money created by the public sector (government jobs and entitlements) and the private sector?

Democrats, Liberals, Progressives, Socialists and some "inside the beltway" Republicans do not think so. To them, all money spent in the economy contributes to the size of the Gross Domestic Product (the sum of all goods and services taking place in a single calendar year). Therefore, if the economy is slow, government should pour more money into the economy to speed it up.

Seems reasonable enough. Unfortunately, the puzzle is not as simple as it might first appear. There is a difference, a very significant difference, between how money spent in the public sector impacts prosperity and how money spent in the private sector builds wealth.

The Private Sector is driven by profitability and necessity to survive. Even charities and non-profits know they must at least generate cash flow or cease to exist. This creates very important driving factors:
1. If survival depends on profitability, or at least cash flow, there are only three ways to create or improve it:
   a. Increase revenue faster than expenses
   b. Decrease expenses
   c. Increase efficiency - get more done on the same costs
2. Build the future.
   a. Who is your market?
   b. What do they want?
   c. What are they willing to pay for it?

3.   Create lifelong customers and trading partners.
    a. Make sure the trades are "fair" to all parties
    b. Make sure the services meet or exceed all expectations
    c. Keep improving the value of the experience of trades

The private sector both serves and creates the market's need. The market can be as simple as the broad variety of goods and services consumers need or want, or as complex as advanced technology and manufacturing requirements of large corporations. In all cases, it is THE MARKETPLACE that determines what, how much, when, how frequently, and what are the values of these trades.

The private sector naturally creates an environment where better goods and services are provided for lower costs and fees. Let's show two examples:

1.   *Personal Computers*
    ■ In 1984, home Personal Computers began their stratospheric rise in sales. At that time the favorite model, the IBM PC, came with an 8-bit by 16-bit single processor, two floppy disks, a black and white monitor that had 640 by 480 pixels, and 128 k of RAM. It cost on the average around $3,000. In today's inflated currency that would be about $10,000!
    ■ Today, a Dell or Hewlett Packard PC comes with four 64-bit processors; it also has 8 Gigabits of RAM, a 1 Terabyte data storage system, and full-color monitor with resolutions over 1600 pixels by 1200 pixels. You can purchase one for under $800, around $267 in 1984 money.

2.   *Personal Massage*
    ■ In the late 1990s and early 2000s the personal massage industry began to grow. Depending on the training and skill of the masseuse, you would pay between $85 and $125 for a one-hour massage.
    ■ Today, a national franchise organization, Massage Envy, provides high quality trained masseuses to consumers for around $55 per hour, and in some cases, less to regular members. In today's inflation, this would be the equivalent of paying about $38 an hour in 1998.

Does this mean that these two industries are in decline? After all, lower prices, less profitability? Just the opposite is true.

Personal Computers have a life span of about three years. Lowering the price has created a significantly larger customer base; not only do lower income families now have computers, many of them have more than one!

Twenty years ago, the idea of a monthly massage was a dream only available to the wealthy. Today, most middle class households can easily afford them and the physical benefits they provide in a very stressful world.

The private sector not only naturally provides more-better-faster goods and services, it also allows the market to buy and sell at its own pace. This is important, as when the market knows or senses it is getting great value for the things it needs or wants, it engages in more trades. More trades mean that the trades happen at a faster rate.

The Velocity of Money

The pace and frequency at which trades happen is called The Velocity of Money. It is probably the most important factor in our economic health. The reason? As the velocity increases, several things occur:

1. There are more trades.
2. More trades results in more "taxable" activities – that is, tax revenue RISES for government.
3. More trades also results in more jobs, as there is an increased need to provide the goods and services the market is demanding.
4. Lower unemployment means we can absorb more people into the workforce. This is great news for legal immigrants!
5. Lower unemployment also means there is a lower demand on certain types of entitlements such as food stamps, welfare, and unemployment compensation benefits.
6. That reduces the federal budget expenditures.

The private sector growing The Velocity of Money is VERY GOOD for our economy! It follows The Golden Rules of Economics by allowing True Capitalism to flourish.

The Public Sector is very different. There are many reasons for federal government employees beyond the military, national defense, foreign relations, international trade, and the people who support our courts and Congress. There will always be federal government employees, but as long as the federal government sticks to what its Constitutional responsibilities are, Congress can control their spending.

Unfortunately, today's reality is far from under control. Citizens must understand:

- Government is a monopoly. It has no concern about competitiveness or efficiency.
- Most government agencies and their employees do not produce or create things that the market requires, unless the Government has taken over a free market service. Think of the debate after 9/11 about whether the TSA should be fulfilled by the private sector or by the government.
- Regulatory agencies that report to the White House add significant expenses to the private sector's ability to conduct business.

What actually happens to the money spent by the Federal Government? A practical way to think of this is to split government spending into two categories.

1. Spending in the Bureaucracy – Most of the federal budget is spent on a combination of entitlements (Medicaid, Medicare, etc.), wages and benefits, retirement plans, and a large variety of miscellaneous expenses[lvii] such as advertising,[lviii] public relations, events, and so on…

2. Spending into the Private Sector – Some of the federal budget is spent on products that are used by the federal government. Think of the military's equipment, weapons, food and munitions. Also think of the desks, refrigerators, air conditioning units, computers and other "stuff" that it takes to run the country.

In Chapter 7 I reviewed Government Spending in the Bureaucracy. Let's do a quick summary:

- Lots of vacation
- 13 paid sick days per year, on top of vacation days
- Flexible work schedules
- Telework
- Programs for child care and elder care

- Subsidies and dependent care flexible spending accounts
- Employee assistance programs
- 401K plans are matched up to 5% of employees contribution.
- Government health benefits have about 350 health plan options throughout the United States. At least a dozen are available to each employee.
- Dental and vision are also available to employees, retirees and their eligible family members.
- Flexible spending accounts for health care are also available.
- Pay incentives for relocation, retention and recruitment for certain positions.
- Special consideration for student loan repayment.
- Postal workers pay considerably less for their health benefits than competitive federal civil service employees due to negotiated contracts.
- Salaries: Federal workers were awarded bigger average pay and benefit increases than private employees for nine years in a row. The compensation gap between federal and private workers has doubled in the past decade.
- Federal civil servants earned average pay and benefits of $123,049 in 2009 while private workers made $61,051 in total compensation.
- The federal compensation advantage has grown from $30,415 in 2000 to $61,998 in 2009.

What does all this mean? Employees of the federal government are far better off than similar private sector workers. They get longer vacations, better retirement and pensions, and almost no jeopardy of competition for their jobs. They get automatic cost of living pay increases.

They do not operate in a system anything like the private sector.

It is important to understand what motivates all people at their core before evaluating them in their circumstances. This means we are not judging how people behave in situations they find themselves, only understanding both "why" they behave the way they do, and "what" the consequences are of that behavior.

Maslow's Theory (Chapter 2) is clear about how once survival and provision are experienced, love, belonging and personal esteem can grow. This is true whether you are in the private or public sector. The difference lays in what brings it about.

In the public sector a person's survival, provision, and so on are very close to being fully guaranteed. They do not depend on profitability, competition, the economy, marketplace, changing culture, foreign trade, or any other factors that directly impact a person's survival in the private sector.

As our economy worsens by violating all The Golden Rules of Economics, everyone gets fearful. After all, survival is being threatened. This is true both in the public and private sector. The public sector is fearful their budgets will be cut (or not allowed to increase), and the private sector is fearful that they cannot survive the overwhelmingly increasing demands of the public sector.

Here is the hub of the issue. People in the public sector are:
- Driven to survival
- Not driven to survive due to competition from other job candidates
- Driven to increase their personal income
- Not driven to increase personal income through profitability
- Driven to protect their lifestyle
- Not driven to protect their lifestyle through improving efficiency

In fact, most people in the federal public sector can create a life experience very similar to that of a child in a very wealthy family: a life that is safe, protected, comfortable, and always wanting a little more.

Plain facts that result from these truths:
1. Costs for services provided by the public sector are much higher than costs for identical services provided by the private sector in an open market (meaning not awarded; no Washington Inc.).
2. Pay scales for public sector jobs far exceed equivalent private sector pay scales.
3. There is little motivation for the public sector to improve efficiency.
4. The federal public sector is guaranteed both pay increases and budget increases every year without accountability to Congress.

5. Additional legislation from Congress and increasing regulatory laws from the White House have relentlessly increased the size of the federal public sector (both in employees and in costs) for over 50 years[lix] with no end in sight.

Now let's look at how spending by the federal government into the private sector works.

Opportunities to win a government contract are greatly cherished by private business. There is a sense the government will always pay for what it receives. The Requests For Proposals (RFPs), are large, complex and have to account for many details typically not seen in the private sector.

Most companies submitting RFPs to the federal government make sure there is plenty of "protection" in the offering. This means you see bids for toilet seats for the Army costing $400, or $197 hammers. There are many reasons for this, but it drives up costs to government, and by that, to taxpayers.

There is another challenge with RFPs to the federal government. Many are provided by such a limited number of private sector providers that there is little actual competition. Dwight David Eisenhower, president from 1952 to 1960, disliked this element of the economy the most. He referred to it as the "Military/Industrial Complex."[lx] He knew it was costly beyond belief, and completely lacking in competition or efficiency.

The final challenge with RFPs is in many cases (think the ½ billion dollar loan to Solyndra),[lxi] the contract is not at all fair to a free market. It is a "favor" from government to companies that support politicians or people in high positions of the administration. It is Mercantilism, or in today's language, **Washington Inc.**

So why doesn't additional spending from the public sector improve the economy?

Let's look again at the two ways the money is spent.

Spending in the bureaucracy constantly rises without real motivation for efficiency, improvement of services, or any true contribution to the economy.

Think of the cost of 82,420 pages of regulatory law in 2011.[lxii] [lxiii] Is that a contribution to what the marketplace is seeking, or just another cost passed on to the economy, paid for by taxpayers? Spending in the bureaucracy only adds additional tax burden to the private sector, as the general population would not ask for all the programs becoming part of the federal landscape.

Again: There is and always will be a need for departments in government. This includes military, infrastructure, foreign affairs, intelligence and other disciplines.

Most of these generate need for the federal government to do business with the private sector. This will not usually be efficient or under budget.

The reasons the economy does not benefit?
1. The public sector inherently cannot improve its efficiency or quality of services. It historically winds up providing less while costing more.
2. The public sector will always have a voracious appetite for growth.
3. Most people who work in the public sector have little grasp of life in the private sector or understanding of how it operates.
4. The public sector does not engage in trades the private sector requests. In other words it is an *enforced* trade, not a free trade.
5. This means the public sector, both out of necessity (as government is a form of monopoly), and out of the life experience working in it provides, does not engage in the true definition of Capitalism: *an economic system of barter in which all trading partners believe they receive equal or greater return in exchange for what they give up.*
6. The lack of efficiency in government results in fewer benefits for every increasing cost; this slows down the Velocity of Money.
7. Most importantly, the tax burden created by the public sector primarily comes from the private sector. This increases the cost of living with no additional benefit to taxpayers.
8. A slower Velocity of Money means fewer opportunities to collect taxes, which means LESS MONEY for the government to spend. This is one of many reasons the federal government must borrow 60% of every dollar it spends.

I am reminded of the children's fairy tale about the goose that laid the golden egg.

The Goose That Laid the Golden Egg
An Aesop Fable

A man and his wife owned a very special goose. Every day the goose would lay a golden egg, which made the couple very rich.

"Just think," said the man's wife, "If we could have all the golden eggs that are inside the goose, we could be richer much faster."

"You're right," said her husband, "We wouldn't have to wait for the goose to lay her egg every day."

So, the couple killed the goose and cut her open, only to find that she was just like every other goose. She had no golden eggs inside of her at all, and they had no more golden eggs.

The public sector lives off the taxes created primarily by the private sector. Just like *The Goose That Laid The Golden Egg*, the public sector lives very well, indeed by the "gold" created by the private sector.

Unfortunately, we have reached the point where, much like the man and his wife, the public sector is about to kill the private sector's ability to lay "golden eggs."

As Maggie Thatcher pointed out, *"The problem with socialism is that eventually you run out of other people's money to spend…"*

The Golden Rules of Economics in Washington Inc.
- Washington Inc. is NOT Capitalism: it is a monopoly that has run beyond reason in its brutal effects on the U.S. economy.
- Washington Inc. is Kleptonomics: it is the federal government forcing unwanted trades at unreasonable levels on the private sector.

So, how are you feeling about your own personal trades with the federal government?

THE GOLDEN RULES OF ECONOMICS

13 BREAKING THE GOLDEN RULES OF ECONOMICS IN PROGRESSIVES AND LIBERALS

Who are Progressives?

The Progressive movement began in the early part of the 20ᵗʰ Century with Teddy Roosevelt.ˡˣⁱᵛ It was supported by the growing list of intellectuals focused on order, community, neighborhood stability, and social justice - things that the industrial society had changed.ˡˣᵛ

Teddy's political platform focused on social and political reform. His movement was the birthplace for what we know today as the Dept. of Health and Human Services, Medicare and Medicaid, OSHA, inheritance taxes, Environmental Protection Agency and The Department of Education.ˡˣᵛⁱ This was the start of a "big government" strategy that would touch every American's life through government regulations and entitlements. It also gave governmental power to career politicians who viewed government as the solution to social injustice and unequal incomes.

Other politicians adopted and expanded the Progressive movement along with its costs and regulatory programs. Presidents such as Franklin D. Roosevelt, Lyndon Johnson and Jimmy Carter supported and expanded the movement into bigger, more costly social programs like the New Deal,ˡˣᵛⁱⁱ the Great Society,ˡˣᵛⁱⁱⁱ and the Departments of Energyˡˣⁱˣ and Education.ˡˣˣ All of these programs and departments increased the size of government and role government plays in how we live and what we earn.

With the increased size of our government came the need for people to enforce and oversee these programs. Departments full of non-elected bureaucrats grew, as regulations were written with requirements to check on the enforcement of the regulations. Do you get the feeling Progressivism means there are more people looking over your shoulder and into your home?

So how big are these Progressive programs today, and how many people are involved in supporting these programs, agencies and departments?

Health and Human Services – In budget year 2011, they had a total budget authority of nearly $902 billion, and over 72,900 (full-time equivalent) employees.[lxxi]

Department of Energy – In 2011 had over 116,000 employees and contractors' total liabilities of $371 billion, including $30.3 billion in pension and related liabilities.[lxxii]

Department of Education – In 2011 spent $69.9 billion.[lxxiii]

Environmental Protection Agency – Over 17,000 employees at a cost of $320 million.[lxxiv]

According to a *USA Today* article from 2010, the government spent in 2008 about $224 billion on salaries for about 2 million civilian employees. The article also stated that in a wide range of jobs, federal employees earn higher average salaries than private sector workers doing the same job.[lxxv]

Do you think costs have gone up since 2008? Have your wages and benefits gone up by the same amount?

Remember, government does not:
- Grow crops
- Raise cattle
- Build small businesses
- Build factories

They do, however, pay their workers more and have better benefits and pensions than private sector companies… and WE pay for this.

What is the real truth about this? The injustices of "big business" are *nothing* compared to big government. At least private business is producing *something of economic value that can be sold or traded when both parties believe they each receive equal or greater value – True Capitalism.*

This is no longer big government; this is HUGE government. The "haves" are the government employees and politicians. Who are the "have-nots"? We, the people of these United States…

I recently read a poster that said, *Government: If you think the problems we create are bad, just wait until you see our solutions.*[lxxvi]

72

A Lesson from the Jamestown Settlers

How far back does the lesson of Progressive thinking go? Is the idea of the government deciding how to create "fairness" in the community a new idea?

The first American settlers living in Jamestown had fertile soil to plant crops, an abundance of wild game, and fruits of many kinds all around them. Yet in a mere six months all but 38 of the original 104 had died due to famine. Two years later, when 500 more people were sent to settle in Virginia, 440 died within six months. Why did this happen with wild game and fertile land around them?

How Capitalism Saved America by Thomas J. DiLorenzo, sheds light on this painful story when he quotes the writings of one eyewitness, *"The cause of starvation was want of providence, industrie and government not the barennesse and defect of the Countrie, as is generally supposed."*[lxxvii]

All they produced went into a common pool, compensating the Virginia Company for their free passage to the New World. The settlers had no ownership. *"The absence of property rights - and of the work/reward nexus that such rights create - completely destroyed the work ethics of the settlers."*[lxxviii]

The studies of economic historians Gary Walton and Hugh Rockoff indicate that when workers have no property rights and shirkers can free-ride on the labor of others, the incentive to produce is lost.[lxxix]   Apathy and lethargy from lack of personal ownership and reward were literally killing the settlers.

Ultimately, the British government sent Sir Thomas Dale to the Virginia colony. He observed that while most settlers had starved to death, the remaining ones spent much of their time playing games in the street, rather than addressing their impending personal crisis. He identified that the system of communal ownership was the problem.

There is an instinctive need in people to reap the fruit of their labors and engage in fair trade. Dale directed that each man be given his own property, and be required to work only one month of the year to contribute to the treasury of the colony. Through ownership of private property and incentives to work hard, the colony turned around. The introduction of a Capitalist system saved the settlers.[lxxx]

The impact on Americans today of uncontrolled taxpayer-funded assistance is similar to the experience of the early Virginia colonists. Unsuccessful attempts to eliminate poverty through government assistance programs enables those receiving aid to stop working hard on their own behalf.

In 2009, food subsidy programs such as food stamps, school breakfast and lunch programs, and Women, Infants and Children (WIC) program cost taxpayers $79 billion. There are approximately 26 food and nutrition programs being operated by six different agencies for the federal government. Furthermore, food subsidy programs are fraught with fraud, keeping state workers busy verifying accurate information.[lxxxi]

Today we see recipients of Food Stamps able to use their Electronic Benefits Transfer (EBT) Cards for years and years. One young woman who cashiered at Wal-Mart during college writes, *"A man showed me his welfare card for I.D. to buy alcohol ... I was born in 1991. The man had been on welfare my entire life."*[lxxxii] This young woman cites many additional examples of misuse of EBT cards and Temporary Assistance for Needy Families she observed during her employment at Wal-Mart.

Senator Mike Carrell (R) from Washington State has created a bill addressing numerous abuses of EBT cards, such as using EBTs in strip clubs, tattoo parlors, and even selling them on *Craigslist.com*.[lxxxiii] Senator Carrell's bill, introduced in March 2011, was still pending as of January 9, 2012.[lxxxiv]

Even the emergency food program that provided disaster funds for families impacted by Tropical Storm Irene during the summer of 2011 was subject to abuse and fraud by state employees who misrepresented information on their applications for food stamps.[lxxxv]

Some of today's financial assistance recipients, like the Virginia settlers, have lost the incentive to produce for themselves. That which was meant to help (public assistance), actually *enslaves* people in a lifestyle lacking the fulfillment of basic human needs such as self-esteem, or becoming productive contributors to society.

Entitlement programs create disincentives both for the recipients and the productive citizens who work hard. Tax dollars pay for programs that are often wasteful and do not break the cycle of poverty. Truly caring for the needy must include helping them provide for themselves so they can have fulfilling lives.

So, what have we discovered?

The Golden Rules of Economics in Progressives and Liberals
- Factual evidence of history, the state of today's world, and actual life experiences do not support beliefs of Progressives and Liberals.
- Progressive and Liberal beliefs violate the basic human instinct of True Capitalism. By doing so, they rob and cheat both those from whom they take personal rewards, and those upon whom they bequeath them.
- Progressives and Liberals believe they understand what individuals need, and how to give it to them, better than the individuals themselves.
- Like all tyrannies, Progressives and Liberals integrate their beliefs into the educational system and mainstream media to indoctrinate others into their beliefs.

In other words, Progressive beliefs and the government policies that come from them, break The Golden Rules of Economics.

Do you feel cheated in the trade yet?

14 THE GOLDEN WAY OUT, PART 1

For those of us who enjoy watching movies created during the Golden Age of Hollywood, (or those of us old enough to remember), Oliver Hardy frequently told Stanley Laurel, *"Well, here's another nice mess you've gotten me into!"* Somehow in Hardy's mind, it was always Laurel who got them into the mess.

We are fast approaching the time when the collective results (and consequences) of more than 60 years of violating The Golden Rules of Economics will become as undeniable to all of us as they were to Oliver Hardy. Only this time, slapstick comedy will not rescue us. Just as Oliver believed Stanley caused the problems, in fact it was Oliver's bumbling leadership combined with Stanley's inability to speak (or get Oliver to listen to him) that led to disaster.

Today, most people are either unaware of what is really going on (Hardy's position), or too frightened, unwilling, or unable to get others to listen (Laurel's position). There are many reasons people may be unaware:
- They work in the public sector.
- They work for the public sector.
- They are a member of a union in a state that does not have "right to work" laws so their incomes and stability are not based on efficiency, profitability and competition.
- The educational system has indoctrinated them into beliefs rather than teaching them to think and decide on their own.
- Their sources of public and private information are carefully crafted with bias; they live by highly sophisticated propaganda.
- Their lives are challenged at Maslow's most basic levels - survival and protection/provision. It is all they can do to survive.
- Their beliefs have become so indoctrinated that facts have no impact on them.
- And many more…

Likewise, why are those who see what is happening so unable to speak?
- They might lose their jobs if they say anything.

- They are part of a union in a state that does not have "right to work" laws. Saying something would have bad consequences.
- They feel they are in the minority; what good would saying anything do?
- They sense the problems, but don't know how to speak about them plainly.
- They learn talking points that only appeal to those who already believe and agree with them.
- They are afraid to become active.
- They are used to being bullied; they do not fight back.
- And much more…

We are at a point in our nation's history wherein if we are to survive, the times of Laurel and Hardy must pass. It is not enough for people to arm-chair quarterback, blame others, or remain passive. Every one of us must get very active on which candidates get elected, policies we insist they put into action, and how we will keep them actively accountable while in office. No one can remain idle; this is no longer "situation comedy America." This is a nation in grave peril, and frankly, the rest of the world hangs in the balance.

In the next series of chapters I will lay out what I believe must happen through the next White House and Congress to turn our nation around. It will not be painless. It will not transform us instantly. It will not be without sacrifice. Those who survive on the backs of other Americans will be angry, outraged and loud. These truths must only strengthen our resolve. The Revolutionary War that founded our nation - the financial war against enslavement of our citizens by its government - has not ended. We MUST end it over these next four election cycles.

15 THE GOLDEN WAY OUT, PART 2

The 1950s were, by and large, a good time economically for the United States. The rest of the world was ravaged by World War II. Europe had not recovered as a manufacturing stronghold, Japan was crippled by the consequences of nuclear annihilation and total surrender, China was suffering under the slaughterhouse regime of Mao Tse Tung, and the Korean War crippled the people ravaged by Japan just a decade earlier.

Although WW II had a heavy price, we were "the last man standing." United States manufacturing, agriculture, electronics, energy, and services were the benchmark of the world. The Cold War drove expansion and growth of the military, and led to incredible technology fueled by space exploration. All this drove an enviable international balance of trade.

The balance of trade is simple to understand. You take the total value/purchase price of all goods and services imported to the United States and subtract that from the total value/purchase price of all goods and services exported from the United States. If you have a positive number, the country is in a good economic position. You are selling more than you are buying. That means you have money left over, and money left over results in building wealth as a nation.

This did not mean all things were good economically. Dwight D. Eisenhower, President from 1952 to 1960, was a lifetime military officer, not a private sector citizen. Although he ran for office as a Republican, that was strictly an act of convenience; Eisenhower at best was politically neutral. Perhaps one of the most chilling economic consequences of Eisenhower's term in office was how he considered certain sectors of our economy as critical to national defense. This means that during his term the federal government regulated entire sectors of the economy. The rationale for this activity was an attempt by the government to limit so-called monopolies by very large companies, and resulted from Supreme Court antitrust rulings during earlier parts of the 20th Century.

What did "regulating a sector of the economy" mean? It meant each year companies doing business in those sectors were required to submit their financial records to the federal government - to bureaucrats. Oversight included federal subsidies, tax advantages, inspection, standards of quality, and a host of other "concerns for the citizens of the United States." Among these, for many of the industries, regulating agencies would also determine:

1. "Average" costs of all those companies to run their businesses.
2. What the federal government believed should be an acceptable average profit.
3. From this, the federal government would determine the price of the goods and services.

Which sectors of the U.S. economy were regulated?
- Transportation - including railroads, trucking and airlines
- Banking
- Radio and television
- Natural gas[lxxxvi]
- Electric utilities[lxxxvii]
- Interstate commerce[lxxxviii]
- Agriculture[lxxxix]
- Food and drugs[xc]
- Alcohol, tobacco and firearms[xci]

Think about it: if you knew someone else was going to determine an "acceptable" level of profit, and tell you what you must charge for your product, do you think you might be a little "generous" in recording of your expenses? Do you think labor unions would be driven to work harder and be more efficient in the operation of their businesses?

The effect was easy to spot. In particular, there were many bits of "folklore wisdom" on many industries. Automobiles were a common one. The auto industry of that day wound up with curious anachronisms for their vehicles:

Ford: **F**ix **O**r **R**epair **D**aily
Plymouth: **P**lease **L**eave **Y**our **M**oney **O**ut **U**nder **T**he **H**ood
JEEP: **J**ust **E**ats **E**very **P**art
Chevrolet: **C**heap **H**eap, **E**very **V**alve **R**attles, **O**il **L**eaks **E**very **T**ime

Dodge: **D**rips **O**il **D**rops **G**rease **E**verywhere

An actual personal concern was hoping your car was not built on a Monday or Friday. On Monday, too hung over; on Friday, everyone hustling to take the weekend off.

Despite this, the United States was considered the highest quality manufacturing country in the world. Cadillac justifiably was regarded as "The Standard of the World." National Cash Register (NCR), International Business Machines (IBM), and General Electric were global "benchmark" companies. At that time "Made In Japan" was a cruel statement, implying that the product would probably self-destruct on the first day of ownership.

How then could the nation wind up so prosperous during that time?

There were numerous reasons, but the largest of them included:
1. Great benefits of the nation's positive balance of trade.
2. Relative global peace; the world was still recovering from the magnitude of WW II.
3. Disposable/consumable costs of living were a low percentage of the cost of living. Average people did not have to spend over 70% of their income on food, utilities, insurance, energy, health care, transportation, education, communications, and taxes as we do today.
4. Expected mortality age of 63 to 65 years old.
5. Limited size of entitlement programs, at least for a while.

During the 1950s, entitlement programs were small and narrow in scope. These included:
- Social Security
- Federal/state unemployment benefits

In 1950, 61 percent of civilian workers were in jobs covered by Social Security, but by 1959 the figure exceeded 86 percent.[xcii] Unemployment benefits were limited, with each state having a program jointly funded from state taxes and the collection of money by the IRS.

How times changed in the 1960s! Several key events occurred during a short stretch of time that changed the shape of our nation beyond what anyone at the time could imagine. The first was escalation of the Cold War, brought about by the crisis in Cuba.

A short summary of The Bay of Pigs and the Cuban Missile Crisis:

January 3, 1961: The U.S. terminates diplomatic and consular relation with Cuba.

April 12, 1961: President Kennedy pledges the U.S. will not intervene militarily to overthrow Castro.

April 17, 1961: Backed by the U.S., a group of Cuban exiles invades Cuba at the Bay of Pigs in an attempt to trigger an anti-Castro rebellion. The invasion fails: Castro's forces capture more than a thousand Cuban rebels.

June 3-4, 1961: Khrushchev and Kennedy hold a summit in Vienna.

July 27, 1962: Castro announces that Cuba is taking measures that would make any direct U.S. attack on Cuba the equivalent of a world war. He claims the U.S.S.R. has invested greatly in helping defend his country.

August 10, 1962: CIA Director John McCone sends a memo to Kennedy expressing his belief that Soviet medium-range ballistic missiles will be deployed in Cuba.

August 31, 1962: Senator Kenneth Keating tells the Senate there is evidence of Soviet missile installations in Cuba. Keating urges Kennedy to take action.

September 11, 1962: In a speech to the UN, Soviet Foreign Minister Andrei Gromyko warns that an American attack on Cuba could mean war with the Soviet Union.

October 9, 1962: Kennedy orders a U-2 reconnaissance flight over western Cuba, delayed by bad weather until the 14th.

October 10, 1962: Senator Keating charges that six intermediate-range ballistic missile bases are being constructed in Cuba.

October 14, 1962: A U-2 flying over western Cuba discovers missile sites. Photographs obtained by this flight provide hard evidence that Soviets have missiles in Cuba.

October 15, 1962: A readout team at the National Photographic Intelligence Center reviews photos taken during the U-2 flight and identifies objects similar to MRBM components observed in the U.S.S.R. at San Cristobal. McGeorge Bundy decides after hearing about the discovery of missiles in Cuba not to inform the president until the next day. McNamara is shown the photographic evidence of the Medium Range Ballistic Missiles (MRBMs) at San Cristobal.

October 16, 1962: Bundy breaks the news to Kennedy, who calls for a meeting of a group later to become known as EX-COMM. At that meeting Kennedy and his advisors discuss possible diplomatic and military courses of action.

October 17, 1962: Kennedy flies to Connecticut to campaign for the Democratic Party and congressional candidate Abraham Ribicoff. Robert Kennedy and Theodore Sorensen meet the President at the airport and fill him in on what he had missed during that day's deliberations. Throughout EX-COMM's discussions, the Joint Chiefs of Staff and especially the Air Force strongly argue for an air strike. After another U-2 flight on the night of the 17th, the military discovers Intermediate Range Ballistic Missiles (IRBMs) designed to carry SS-5 nuclear warheads.

October 18, 1962: Gromyko and Kennedy meet for two hours. Reading from notes, Gromyko assures Kennedy that Soviet aid to Cuba has been only for the "defensive capabilities of Cuba."

October 19, 1962: Kennedy departs Washington for scheduled campaign speeches in Cleveland and the West Coast.

October 20, 1962: Kennedy's Press Secretary announces that the President is canceling the remainder of his campaign trip because of an "upper respiratory infection." Kennedy meets with his advisors and orders a defensive quarantine instituted as soon as possible. The full operation is reviewed and approved, and the President's television address is scheduled for the next evening.

October 21, 1962: Kennedy is told by General Maxwell Taylor that an air strike could not guarantee to destroy all Soviet missiles in Cuba. Kennedy decides on a quarantine of Cuba for the time being. Kennedy requests that the press not deny him the "element of surprise" or he warns, "I don't know what the Soviets will do." Another U-2 flight that day reveals bombers and MIGs being rapidly assembled and cruise missile sites being built on Cuba's northern shore.

October 22, 1962: Congressional leaders assemble at the White House for a meeting with Kennedy. They are shown the photographic evidence of the Soviet missile installations. The congressional leaders express support, but many advocate stronger action. The President addresses the nation in a televised speech, announcing the presence of offensive missile sites in Cuba. U.S. military forces go to DEFCON 3. Marines reinforce U.S. base at Guantanamo Bay.

October 23, 1962: Kennedy orders six Crusader jets to fly a low-level reconnaissance mission. The Organization of American States (OAS) unanimously approves of the quarantine against Cuba. By the end of the day U.S. ships had taken up position along the quarantine line, 80 miles from Cuba. Late in the evening, the President sends Robert Kennedy to the Soviet embassy to talk with Ambassador Dobrynin. Kennedy receives a letter from Khrushchev in which Khrushchev comments that there is a "serious threat to peace and security of peoples." President Kennedy decides to give Khrushchev more time and pulls the quarantine line back to 500 miles.

October 24, 1962: Soviet ships en route to Cuba with questionable cargo either slow down or reverse their courses except for one. Military forces go to DEFCON 2, the highest ever in U.S. history.

October 25, 1962: Kennedy sends a letter to Khrushchev laying the responsibility for the crisis on the Soviet Union. EX-COMM discusses a proposal to withdraw U.S. missiles from Turkey in exchange for the withdrawal of Soviet missiles in Cuba.

October 26, 1962: The Soviet ship Marucla is cleared through the quarantine. During an EX-COMM meeting, Kennedy says he believes the quarantine alone cannot force the Soviet government to remove its offensive weapons from Cuba. A CIA report that morning states there was no halt in progress in development of the missile sites, and another reconnaissance flight reveals the Soviets also attempting to camouflage the missiles. Aleksandr Fomin, known to be the KGB station chief in Washington, requests a meeting with ABC News correspondent John Scali. Fomin proposes dismantling of Soviet bases under U.N. supervision in exchange for a public pledge from the U.S. not to invade Cuba. Khrushchev sends another letter to Kennedy proposing removing his missiles if Kennedy would publicly announce never to invade Cuba.

October 27, 1962: An American U-2 is shot down over Cuba killing the pilot, Major Rudolf Anderson. A U-2 accidentally strays into Soviet airspace near Alaska and is nearly intercepted by Soviet fighters. Dobrynin and Robert Kennedy meet and discuss the price of removing the missiles from Cuba. Kennedy writes Khrushchev a letter stating he will make a statement that the U.S. will not invade Cuba if Khrushchev removes the missiles from Cuba.

October 28, 1962: On Radio Moscow, Khrushchev announces he has agreed to remove the missiles from Cuba.[xciii]

The impact of this on our economy cannot be underestimated. I remember going through "training" in seventh grade about how to hide under my desk in case of nuclear attack, and subsequent escalation of spending on the military as the Vietnam War began. The Military/Industrial Complex was moving into full swing at the greatest pace since the peak of World War II. The Vietnam War was, in many ways, a direct consequence of the Cuban Missile Crisis.

Our failure in the Vietnam War created an escalation of global hostilities by the Soviet Union and China. Lyndon Baines Johnson's Great Society programs added dimensions and layers to the entitlement world we live in today. This resulted in escalation of spending in national defense, welfare, other entitlement programs, and college loans (which increase the debt of graduating students). This in turn combined with the impact of baby boomers bursting into adulthood, marriage, families and starter homes.

There was a Conservative outrage; Barry Goldwater's rise in the Republican Party was a direct consequence of the welfare state LBJ was creating. Unfortunately, the collusion of both the print and television news with the Democratic Party candidates became institutionalized at this time.

Finally, the unthinkable happened. We wound up on the short side of the balance of trade; we were importing more than we were exporting.

THE GOLDEN RULES OF ECONOMICS

16 THE GOLDEN WAY OUT, PART 3

The Balance of Trade

Let's start with a basic truth. If you spend more than you make, eventually you go broke. If a community spends more money that leaves the community than outside money that comes into the community, the community winds up poor and dependent. If a nation imports more goods and services than it exports, it winds up the financial servant of other nations.

How pitiful that we are in that situation today.

Perhaps our country's largest challenge occurred when in the late 1960s we started the process of becoming dependent on foreign sources of oil for the energy of our nation. For the first time in the history of our nation, our financial stability could be dictated by nations other than us. They raise the price of oil; we pay more. They restrict the volume of oil; we pay more.

The Bureau of the Census also reports the United States experienced its first trade deficit (total of all exports minus total of all imports) of the twentieth century in 1971, with a trade deficit of approximately $1.5 billion. A record high trade deficit occurred in 1998, when imports exceeded exports by approximately $230 billion. This deficit went up again to more than $300 billion in 2000 and it only got worse as the decade rolled on.

Trade Balance – Goods on a Census Basis

Value in Millions of Dollars 1960 – 1998

Year	Balance	Total Exports	Total Imports
1960	4,609	19,626	15,018
1961	5,476	20,190	14,714
1962	4,583	20,973	16,390
1963	5,289	22,427	17,138
1964	7,006	25,690	18,684
1965	5,333	26,699	21,366
1966	3,830	29,372	25,542

Year	Balance	Total Exports	Total Imports
1967	4,122	30,934	26,812
1968	837	34,063	33,226
1969	1,290	37,332	36,042
1970	3,225	43,176	39,951
1971	-1,476	44,087	45,563
1972	-5,729	49,854	55,583
1973	2,389	71,865	69,476
1974	-3,884	99,437	103,321
1975	9,551	108,856	99,305
1976	-7,820	116,794	124,614
1977	-28,353	123,182	151,534
1978	-30,205	145,847	176,052
1979	-23,922	186,363	210,285
1980	-19,696	225,566	245,262
1981	-22,267	238,715	260,982
1982	-27,510	216,442	243,952
1983	-52,409	205,639	258,048
1984	-106,702	223,976	330,678
1985	-117,711	218,815	336,526
1986	-138,280	227,159	365,438
1987	-152,119	254,122	406,241
1988	-118,526	322,426	440,952
1989	-109,400	363,812	473,211
1990	-101,719	393,592	495,311
1991	-66,723	421,730	488,453
1992	-84,501	448,164	532,665
1993	-115,568	465,091	580,659
1994	-150,630	512,626	663,256
1995	-158,801	584,742	743,543
1996	-170,214	625,075	795,289
1997	-181,488	689,182	870,671
1998	-230,852	682,977	913,828

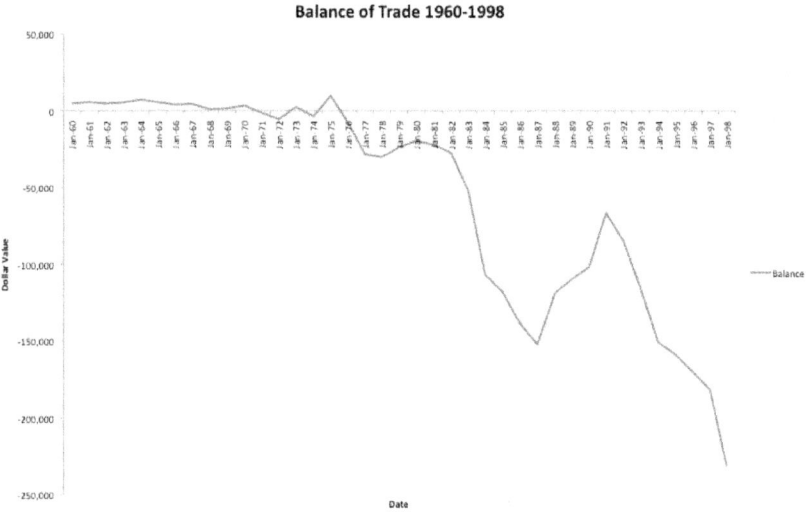

What a sad story. Since 1971 the United States has had only two years of a positive balance of trade...[xciv]

Here is our balance of trade since 1999:

What about oil and gas? In particular, what about our dependence on foreign energy? How much more are we paying out rather than producing on our own and exporting?[xcv]

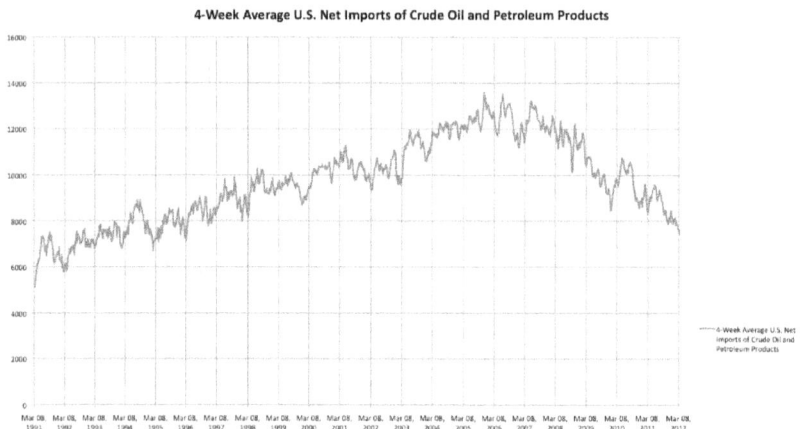

How sad that the real cause of our trade imbalance is not our relationship with China. It is our dependence on foreign oil. Though our annual oil import imbalance has fallen this year to around 9 million barrels per day from a high in 2006-2007 of around 13 million barrels per day, the story is a far more distressing one than just how much of our money gets shipped overseas.

Oil and gas, (and coal for that matter), drive all facets of our U.S. economy. From transportation to energy to heating and cooling, our nation is built around the use of energy.

Most people do not realize that both state and federal governments receive royalties (think "taxes") on oil and gas generation in the United States. So the additional cost of being dependent on foreign energy sources goes far beyond the estimated $55 billion to $327 billion per year we pay to import oil.[xcvi]

Here are some facts. Although the U.S. oil import imbalance in 2012 is about 4 million barrels per day less than in 2007, this is not a sign of economic recovery. During this time the nation was producing more oil than it used as a result of the escalating price of oil (the cost of oil had nearly doubled since early 2007)[xcvii] combined with the recession driving down the use of oil. In other words, the decrease in oil imports is a reflection of how our economy slowed. Escalating oil prices and the recession created a real unemployment rate of around 15%.[xcviii]

Next let's look at consequences of our heavy dependence on foreign oil.

1. Limiting our oil and gas exploration and production freezes the royalties (taxes) paid to the Feds and the States. Bad policy during a time of radical budget deficits, don't you think?

2. $300 billion paid out to foreign nations per year is $300 billion not spent in the United States. This has a larger implication than you think. Money spent in the United States goes through a "multiplier" effect. The same money spent passes through the system multiple times in a year. Each time money is spent it contributes to the economy. How many times it is spent is called "the Velocity of Money," and it is the velocity of money that both creates jobs and increases the taxes the government collects. When the velocity of money slows down there are fewer jobs and fewer taxes. This combines with increased demands on unemployment benefits, food stamps, and other entitlement programs, resulting in certain economic suicide.

3. The unwillingness of Washington to promote expanded energy production means our country has no influence or control over the cost of oil. Supply and demand is very real; larger supply than demand means the price goes down. Small supply and greater demand means the price goes up. What measure of idiocy would drive Washington politicians to allow oil cartels made up of adversarial nations from the Mideast and South America to have a chokehold on our economy?

4. The higher the cost of oil, the higher the cost of everything in the nation. All additional energy and transportation costs have to be added into the price of everything else. Name one item that does not have an "energy" component to it. Retail shopping depends on goods being shipped. Facilities must be heated and cooled. Services

either require transportation to get to the place where they are provided, or electricity to support the technology and telephone systems that carry them. Most of us could not even get to the grocery store simply by walking.

5. Additional oil and gas exploration and production creates many jobs. These jobs go beyond the people who work directly in the energy industry, and include the increase in goods and services – from food to clothing to housing to cars and trucks – that these new workers want and need. More jobs means more money collected by the government, and more money collected by the government during a thriving economy means reducing and eliminating deficits.

Of all the issues outside of uncontrolled government spending, foreign energy dependence is the single largest factor destroying our economy.

What is the way out? Elected officials both at the federal and state levels MUST make energy autonomy one of the cornerstones of their time in office.

Energy autonomy is not the same as energy independence. Technically speaking, if you are consuming less energy than you create, you could argue that you have (at least potentially) energy independence. Energy autonomy goes far beyond energy independence. What are the three attributes of energy autonomy?

1. Open up as much oil and gas exploration in the nation as the marketplace would like. Although it would be several years before actual production occurred in many locations, simply the threat of additional supply will drive the price of oil down. Other providers will want to make it less "attractive" to increase the supply of oil.

2. Quickly reach a point where we are past being dependent on energy imports for our current and growing energy needs, but are actually exporting significant levels of energy to the rising international demand. This turns around our balance of trade problems.

3. Create enough capacity in energy production that we can shape the price of energy globally through increasing or decreasing supply.

That allows us to control our own economy, while helping shape the global economy away from our country's foreign enemies.

Energy Autonomy is the First Rule of the Golden Way Out.

17 THE GOLDEN WAY OUT, PART 4

Health Care

Everyone wants great health care. Health care is probably the third oldest profession after, well, you know, and then politicians... In the not too distant past some practices regarded as great health care actually killed many people. It has only been in the last 65 years that health care, particularly in the United States, has redefined mankind.

Let's take a look at Social Security. When FDR inked the Social Security bill the government had a curious age at which a person qualified for full benefits. The age was 65. Very simple actually; the average life expectancy at that time was 61.7 (59.9 for men and 63.9 for women).[xcix] FDR had no intention of running out of the money people put into Social Security. He anticipated it would pay out far less than it generated. It was a tax revenue scheme.

Look at today: Average life expectancy in the country has gone off the charts. The table beginning on the next page clearly shows this unforeseen trend.

Table 104. Expectation of Life at Birth, 1970 to 2008, and Projections, 2010 to 2020[c]

Beginning 1970, chart excludes deaths of nonresidents of the United States.

Year	Total Age	Male	Female
1960	69.7	66.6	73.1
1970	70.8	67.1	74.7
1971	71.1	67.4	75.0
1972	71.2	67.4	75.1
1973	71.4	67.6	75.3

Year	Total Age	Male	Female
1974	72.0	68.2	75.9
1975	72.6	68.8	76.6
1976	72.9	69.1	76.8
1977	73.3	69.5	77.2
1978	73.5	69.6	77.3
1979	73.9	70.0	77.8
1980	73.7	70.0	77.4
1981	74.1	70.4	77.8
1982	74.5	70.8	78.1
1983	74.6	71.0	78.1
1984	74.7	71.1	78.2
1985	74.7	71.1	78.2
1986	74.7	71.2	78.2
1987	74.9	71.4	78.3
1988	74.9	71.4	78.3
1989	75.1	71.7	78.5
1990	75.4	71.8	78.8
1991	75.5	72.0	78.9
1992	75.8	72.3	79.1
1993	75.5	72.2	78.8
1994	75.7	72.4	79.0
1995	75.8	72.5	78.9
1996	76.1	73.1	79.1
1997	76.5	73.6	79.4
1998	76.7	73.8	79.5
1999	76.7	73.9	79.4
2000	76.8	74.1	79.3
2001	76.9	74.2	79.4
2002	76.9	74.3	79.5
2003	77.1	74.5	79.6

Year	Total Age	Male	Female
2004	77.5	74.9	79.9
2005	77.4	74.9	79.9
2006	77.7	75.1	80.2
2007	77.9	75.4	80.4
2008	77.8	75.3	80.3
Projections			
2010	78.3	75.7	80.8
2015	78.9	76.4	81.4
2020	79.5	77.1	81.9

For a man, life expectancy has risen at least 15 years, since the time of FDR. For a woman, it is at least 16 years. More astonishing is life expectancy of people living to at least 65 years old – it extends to over 82 years in men and 85 years in women.[ci]

That means improvements in health care have added up to 17 to 20 years of government payments to a program intended to pay hardly anyone!

Additionally, improvements in health care become more significant as we get older. The ability to prolong our lives actually becomes a decision based on our choices in health care in our later years.

As health care became more sophisticated it also became more expensive. Research and validation of assumptions and theories take time and resources. Sophisticated equipment was also very costly; after all, unlike automobiles, you are not going to drive the cost down by every year selling 10 million Magnetic Resonance Imaging (MRI) machines costing at least $500,000.

Add to that the myriad of expenses that have become part of health care. They include:[cii]
- Professional care
- Facility costs – inpatient and outpatient
- Administration
- Insurance

- Research and development
- Medications
- Wasted resources and inefficiencies in delivery of care

Let's look at some of the details.

Milliman, an actuarial firm, tracks medical costs using the Milliman Medical Index. This index measures costs for a family of four covered by a traditional employer-provided insurance policy.[ciii] The index shows cost per family increased from $9,235 in 2002 to $19,393 in 2011,[civ] a 110% increase. During that same time, the consumer price index increased only 25%.[cv]

For 2011 the costs break down as follows:[cvi]
- Physician 33%
- Inpatient 31%
- Outpatient 17%
- Pharmacy 15%
- Other services 4%

Think of all the different types of employees there are in a medical facility:
- Nurses
- Laboratory technicians
- Pharmacists
- Physical therapists
- Dietary specialists
- Social workers
- Radiology staff
- Doctors

All these specialists must meet specific educational requirements, be credentialed by a state agency, and participate in continuing education classes. Nursing care alone accounts for 44% of total inpatient costs.[cvii]

Additional staffing includes administrative positions such as day-to-day operations, receptionists, hospital and clinic managers, financial analysis, billing, janitorial, facility maintenance, and other support staff.

Next add the cost of personal liability insurance to both the hospitals and clinics, and to the medical professionals who work in them. For many physicians the cost of this insurance is as large as the personal average incomes of the top 2% of wage earners in our country.[cviii]

Next comes the cost of government. From the federal and state levels right on to third-party regulatory agencies, hospitals must use financial resources to ensure compliance and protect their accreditation.

Beyond these expenses, interest on bonds for capital improvements in facilities and equipment must be paid. Medical supplies, heating, air conditioning, lighting, general grounds and building maintenance, and even public restroom supplies all add to hard dollar costs of running health care facilities.

Another aspect of cost is the inherent inefficiency in the U.S. health care system. Inefficient use of resources may account for more than half of our total health care spending.[cix] Briefly, the top three areas of waste according to a study by PricewaterhouseCoopers' Health Research Institute are:[cx]

- Excessive use of procedures and testing to protect against being sued ($210 billion annually)
- Inefficiency in billing and claims processing (as much as $210 billion annually)
- Patient care related to obesity ($200 billion annually)

Who actually pays these costs? For the average family in 2011 the employer paid $11,385 and the employee paid the balance of $8,008 ($4,728 as employee payroll deduction for health insurance and $3,280 as out-of-pocket expenses).[cxi] The employee's share of total medical expenses for our average family of four has increased faster than the employer's.[cxii] In fact we all pay for the increase in health care indirectly, as it increases the cost of doing business and therefore, raises the cost of goods and services.

All this shows there is a desperate need for real reform in health care in our nation. Many factors play into the reasons for problems in health care. Issues range from lawyers wanting unlimited size settlements on personal liability lawsuits (which results in costly excessive testing by medical professionals who want to protect themselves), to the extremely high cost of medical school, to the constant pressure on paying the real cost of health care services under Medicare and Medicaid.

What about ObamaCare? Wasn't this an attempt on the part of ruling Democrats in the House, Senate, and the White House to reform health care?

If you believe that the legislation rammed down the throats of this country was driven by an attempt to reform health care to the benefit of all Americans, you are more than naïve.

There are many issues with ObamaCare. Whether it is the forced participation (and penalties if you don't) in the legislation that brought about a Supreme Court ruling on its Constitutionality (it was a "tax"), or the panels of bureaucrats who would determine whether you will be allowed to receive health care under the system, the program is a well-documented suicide plan for health care in the U.S. Let's look at some of the real factors:

- *Complexity* – The Department of Health and Human Services has turned **only six pages** of the 907-page law into **429 pages** of new regulations.[cxiii] At this rate, 907 pages translates into 64,850 pages of new regulations!
- *Cost* – More people on Medicaid, federal insurance premium subsidies, and pre-existing condition coverage will all increase overall costs.[cxiv]
- *Government growth* – The Congressional Research Service identified dozens of new government organizations created by ObamaCare, but concluded that the exact number is "unknowable."[cxv]
- *Independent Payment (Medicare) Advisory Board* – Members are appointed by the President, and the Board's purpose is to reduce the growth rate in Medicare costs with no oversight by Congress or the President,[cxvi] **a situation that will likely lead to government rationing of health care to control costs.**
- *Decrease the individual's choice in health care* – The Federal Coordinating Council for Comparative Effectiveness is charged with establishing treatments that are effective.[cxvii] In other words, **federal bureaucrats will determine your treatments, not your doctor.**
- *Decline in private (employment-based) insurance* – The Congressional Budget Office estimates 3 to 5 million fewer people will obtain

coverage through their employer each year from 2019 to 2022 than would have without ObamaCare.[cxviii]
- *The uninsured problem is not solved* – By 2019 there will still be up to 23 million uninsured people.[cxix]

What is the real truth? ObamaCare is nothing more than a brazen attempt on the part of President Obama and Liberal/Democrat/Progressive/Socialists to take over a sixth of the U.S. economy. ObamaCare alone will bankrupt our nation. Don't begin to think that when it is dismantled that the Progressive/Liberals will not try to resurrect it again.

What does real reform look like?
- Reform of Medicare and Medicaid by giving a set amount to individuals in these programs to buy private insurance (voucher system) that controls cost and allows individuals choice of coverage and level of care.
- Reconnect the health care consumer with the health care providers via Health Savings Accounts and high-deductible insurance plans.
- Tax credits for individual health insurance.
- Interstate sale of health insurance promoting competition between health insurers.
- Medical malpractice liability reform.
- High-risk pools at the state level for those who cannot obtain health insurance because of pre-existing conditions.

Those who favor government intrusion into health care in the upcoming election will **increase** the size and complexity of government, **expand** the cost of health care, **ration** health care to control costs, **decrease** individual choice for private insurance, and still **not solve** the problem of the uninsured.

The Money Side

No federal program revealed President Obama's plan for big government dependence and spending more than ObamaCare. While *promising* to reduce the number of "uninsured" without increasing debt, reality tells a story of *staggering* financial impact and *unsound* Constitutional basis.

In stark contrast, the release of the plan by Paul Ryan during his time in the House of Representatives (R-Wis), *"A Roadmap for America's Future Version*

2.0," strikes at the heart of President Obama's big government policies. Ryan's Roadmap is a difference-maker showing that responsible spending can *shrink deficits* and provide greater opportunities. The contrasts cannot be greater, or the stakes higher.[cxx]

ObamaCare's Staggering Economic Impact

With the American people now owing more in federal debt than they earn, the ObamaCare tab is overwhelming and punitive, even for a government-sponsored program.

- **Health care costs continue to climb.** In 1960, health care costs were 5.2% of GDP; in 2010 they were 17.9%.[cxxi] By 2019, the government estimates health care costs will reach 19.4% of GDP.[cxxii]
- **Overall spending has increased.** Annual spending in the Obama years climbed more than 20% to a projected $3.6 trillion in 2012. Previously, government spending averaged 20% of GDP; it is now 24% – without considering ObamaCare.[cxxiii]
- **We owe more than we produce.** With debt levels greater than GDP, our country owes more than we produce each year.[cxxiv] The country is nearly $16 trillion in debt, and will jump to almost $20 trillion by 2015 – without considering ObamaCare.[cxxv]
- **ObamaCare bill will come due.** An in-depth study of the real costs of ObamaCare by Alabama Sen. Jeff Sessions (R) showed a hidden $17 trillion dollar funding gap![cxxvi] According to Sen. Sessions, Senate Budget Committee chairman, ObamaCare will result in this unfathomable funding gap we are committed to spend over the next 10 years. Estimates are based on methods used by the Medicaid and Medicare research center (they report to the White House).[cxxvii]

Supreme Court Takes a Hard Look at ObamaCare

While Obama's Progressive policies take a page from the 1930s New Deal and 1960s Great Society through entitlements and government influence, a sinister side has emerged. Oral arguments for overturning ObamaCare were heard in March 2012 by the Supreme Court as a majority of states (26) filed suit. The strongest Constitutional challenges came from the justices.

Confronting the Constitutional question of ObamaCare's control of the health care market and forcing individual purchase, Justice Scalia used an analogy: *"Everybody has to buy food sooner or later, so you define the market as food, therefore, everybody is in the market; therefore, you can make people buy broccoli."* [cxxviii]

In sharp questioning, Scalia and the other justices *dissected* the ObamaCare *"individual mandate"* sham: If Americans are forced to buy health insurance and the government regulates the purchase of that insurance, we can be forced to buy anything. Where will it stop?[cxxix]

The chilling effect of ObamaCare on the 26 states filing suit was a central concern of the Constitution's writers. Seizing independence from England in an *economic war* was the only course for American colonists trapped by a powerful central government creating unfair trades to benefit the influential few at the expense of the individual. Americans endured law after law impacting their trades... until they hit a *tipping point*. As a result, our leaders created the Constitution with limited federal powers, states rights, and separation of duties between three government branches to protect us from *unlimited powers* of the federal government. Alexander Hamilton said, *"It's not tyranny we desire; it's a just, limited, federal government."* [cxxx]

Either ObamaCare and programs like it, or the Constitution as originally intended will prevail – we cannot have both. The *economic war* is upon the American people as Obama's signature law *requires, for the first time,* purchase of specific insurance. What is next?

Rep. Ryan's Roadmap to Prosperity

With economic "takeover" of the health care industry by the White House and looming financial failure as a backdrop, Paul Ryan's Roadmap presents a compelling case that the President's Progressive policies have brought our country to a *tipping point*.

tipping point — *n*
the crisis stage in a process, when a significant change takes place[cxxxi]

Ryan's plan provides valuable insight into the expanding culture of dependency, proven history of failed Progressive policies, and critical solutions needed to rescue the country from fiscal crisis.

What must be done?

- Elect leaders who will push for real market-based reforms during the next four sessions of Congress.
- Save Medicare and Medicaid by allowing consumers to use vouchers to choose their own coverage.
- From this, use insurance reforms (HSAs and high-deductible plans) to reconnect the consumer of health care with the providers.
- Promote competition in health insurance by allowing interstate sales of health insurance.
- Reform medical liability laws to decrease waste.
- Help those who cannot buy insurance by forming high-risk pools managed at the state level.

Together we can halt the insanity of this current path, a path which will destroy the world's greatest health care system.

Heath Care Reform is the Second Rule of the Golden Way Out.

Note: Deep thanks to Dr. Richard Skoog and Paul Quanrud, without whose research, writing skills and sacrifice this chapter would have been greatly limited.

18 THE GOLDEN WAY OUT, PART 5

The Bureaucracy

Recently I was asked to write a paper on what our current bureaucracy should do to improve efficiency. This means showing all the government agencies that report to the President, all their employees, and all the new czars who have become the Obama White House, what they could be doing to get more done on the same amount of money, or perhaps spending less money. Ignoring the idea that the concept of Bureaucracy and Efficiency is an oxymoron, is there actually a way for them to become more efficient? More importantly, what is the effect of the agencies and czars on our economy, and what is it they contribute?

Perhaps the best place to start is to make a distinction between the public sector (those who are employed by governments at any level) and bureaucrats. The public sector has many jobs that are critical to the working of our nation and communities, and to having a peaceful existence. These jobs include fire departments, law enforcement, the military, the people who work in the judicial system, public parks and recreation, street lighting, and many other small collateral services.

To understand bureaucrats at the national level, you have to understand how many agencies there are. Let's start with the traditional agencies that are represented on the President's Cabinet.[cxxxii] In addition to the Vice President, there is:

1. Agriculture
2. Commerce
3. Defense
4. Education
5. Energy
6. Health and Human Services
7. Homeland Security
8. Housing and Urban Development
9. Interior
10. Labor

11. State
12. Transportation
13. Treasury
14. Veterans Affairs
15. Justice (The Attorney General)

Now let's add in the Czars:^{cxxxiii}
1. The Afghanistan Czar
2. The AIDS Czar
3. The Anti-Semitism Czar
4. The Auto Recovery Czar
5. The Border Czar
6. The California Water Czar
7. The Car and Manufacturing Czar
8. The Central Region Czar (The Middle East, not the Midwest...)
9. The Climate Czar
10. The Domestic Violence Czar
11. The Drug Czar
12. The Economic Czar
13. The Energy and Environment Czar
14. The Faith Based and Neighborhood Partnership Czar
15. The Government Performance Czar
16. The Great Lakes Restoration Czar
17. The Green Jobs Czar
18. The Guantanamo Closure Czar
19. The Health Czar
20. The Information Czar
21. The Intelligence Czar (Foreign Affairs similar to the CIA, not brainpower...)
22. The Mideast Peace Czar
23. The Pay Czar
24. The Regulatory Czar
25. The Safe Schools Czar
26. The Science Czar
27. The Stimulus Accountability Czar
28. The Sudan Czar
29. The TARP Czar
30. The Technology Czar
31. The Terrorism Czar

32. The Urban Affairs Czar
33. The Weapons Czar
34. The Weapons of Mass Destruction Czar

What do you think? Is there any duplicity here between the agencies in the Cabinet and the Czars?

Now how about the additional federal government agencies?[cxxxiv] This would include the Environmental Protection Agency, Government Accountability Office (GAO), and many more. I would like to name them all, but that would be quite a challenge as there are 479 distinct agencies across all three branches of the federal budget – *Yikes!* And this doesn't even include the hundreds of state and local government agencies and offices.[cxxxv]

The regrettable story is that most of these are made up of bureaucrats.

What is the actual definition of a bureaucrat? According to The Free Dictionary[cxxxvi] a bureaucrat is:
1. An official of a bureaucracy.
2. An official who is rigidly devoted to the details of administrative procedure.

In simpler language, a bureaucrat is an employee of a government agency whose job it is to follow procedures and regulations. Can anyone tell me how this contributes to a healthy economy? What roles do bureaucrats play in any social system?

Much as I would like to be cruel, (at least for a moment), it is important to understand that many federal agencies do fulfill critical tasks for our nation. Government does play a crucial role in providing both an environment and needed protections for citizens to live and fulfill their lives by their own choices.

Beyond providing for the common defense, the Preamble to the Constitution says, *"the Federal Government should promote the General Welfare."*[cxxxvii] How does a government "promote" the General Welfare? Progressives and Liberals believe that "promoting" the General Welfare can mean "providing the General Welfare for those who cannot do it on their own," but that is not what the Founding Fathers had in mind.

If you understand that the American Revolution was an economic war against British Mercantilism (Washington Inc. in today's world), it is clear that the objective of the government in General Welfare means two things:

1. Stay out of the way of the open marketplace's ability to engage in trade. In other words, allow true Capitalism to prevail in American Society.
2. Protect citizens and their businesses from unfair trade practices. This includes Mercantilism (unfair trade practices caused by government collusion with business), and improper activities by businesses that result in negative consequences to citizens without their expressed consent. Simple examples might include monopolies, organized crime, and collusion between several businesses in a singular product or service.

If they are driven by these two objectives, and run and managed properly, agencies like the Food and Drug Administration, the firearms and explosives sections of the Bureau of Alcohol, Tobacco, Firearms and Explosives, the FBI, and many other agencies play very important roles in the safety and stability of American society.

Honestly though, 15 departments, 32 Czars, and almost 480 federal agencies; do you think there is any chance for departmental responsibility overlap? There is a reason the federal government represents over 25% of the total U.S. Gross Domestic Product in 2011.[cxxxviii] Keep in mind this does not include state and local government spending!

I hear conservative politicians being outraged at this number, citing that in the past it has usually been about 18%. This drives me batty – why on earth is 18% a "good" number. The inefficiency in government is legendary. Outside a time of war, any number over 15% on the federal level is a guaranteed sign of outrageous waste.

Keep in mind it is not just the budgetary costs of the agencies that are crippling our nation. The number of regulations that exist is so large that it is extremely expensive to fulfill them all. Only the largest companies in the private sector can keep ahead of the regulatory onslaught.

What happens to the hidden costs of this Mount Everest of regulatory law propagated on the private business sector? It is passed on to you, of course.

This cripples our economy and it steals money out of your wallet. Once again, we are forced to pay for a "trade" we had no part in. What is the most horrid effect of the federal bureaucracy? It sets off the chain reaction of:

- Unnecessary expenses
- Rules that limit our ability to provide energy autonomy for the nation
- Costs that are passed on to consumers
- The limiting of the private sector's natural growth, or worse
- The shrinking of the private sector, and by that
- Reducing the taxes that are collected
- Worsening the federal budget deficit

What is the saddest part of all? The pen of the President controls most of this.

So, how do we fix it? What must be done by the next administration (and every one that follows it) to force our way out of the reckless railroad ride straight into the Grand Canyon?

Four key steps must be taken:

1. Dismantling all duplicitous federal agencies. We do not need a Cabinet Level agency, a Czar, and 479 other smaller agencies to fulfill the focus of a larger agency.
2. Take all remaining agency budgets back to 2008 levels.
3. Remove the automatic budget increases in federal programs initiated in the Nixon administration.
4. Set annual performance metrics for each agency. Agencies that do not reach their performance goals will have staff replaced at the top two tiers.

The Dismantling of the Federal Bureaucracy is the Third Rule of the Golden Way Out.

THE GOLDEN RULES OF ECONOMICS

19 THE GOLDEN WAY OUT, PART 6

National Defense and Foreign Policy

I have news for the president: We are no longer in the Cold War.

The Cold War was a unique time in the history of mankind. Never before had there been two enemy nations with the most divergent views of mankind's rights combined with the ability of either of them to destroy the face of the entire earth in a single afternoon. The terror of nuclear war and the threat of communist-totalitarian regimes was the inescapable dark shadow that hung over the earth until the collapse of the Soviet Union during the Reagan-Bush I years.

How times have changed. Today we fight many enemies on many different fronts. The threats to our survival are just as real, and the consequences are just as dark, but our challenge is, "What good is a knife in a fight when your enemy has a loaded automatic weapon?"

Let's first review how World War II was fought.

The first key element was a relentless investment by Germany in new technologies and weapons. Germany's advanced tanks rolled over Eastern Europe and Northern Africa. Few people in the current generation realize that in World War II, Germany had fighter jet planes and the Allies had only propeller driven aircraft. Germany was developing rockets delivering powerful bombing attacks; there was no defense. Beyond this, Germany was developing the nuclear bomb.

What about the role of energy? Was it a factor in all of this? What brought about the defeat of Germany in World War II? Hitler knew his time was limited because of his lack of access to fuel – Germany was lacking the gasoline, diesel, and jet engine fuel to power the army. It was one of the reasons the Allied assault to remove the Nazis from the Middle East was so important.

What about the price paid to even establish a beachhead in Europe? France was occupied. The Nazi bombing runs were pummeling Great Britain. Until the United States decided to enter the war and bring soldiers over to the Allies, Winston Churchill had to stand fearlessly before his people and repeatedly declare, "Never give up! **NEVER NEVER NEVER GIVE UP!**"

The invasion at Normandy was perilous at best. Months of subterfuge to persuade the Nazis that the Allies would mount an invasion from a different location was a critical part of the plan. Even though this deception worked, the toll on the brave souls landing would be great. General Eisenhower KNEW he was sending thousands of soldiers to a certain grave.

On Thanksgiving after 9/11 I flew my wife to Paris. It was the first Thanksgiving ever that none of our children or their families would be with us at home. While there we went on a dinner/dancing cruise on the Seine. We shared a table with a wonderful and gracious French couple, perhaps 20 years older than us. As the conversation progressed from how grateful I was that the French were the first to stand with the United States in the outrage and conflict with Radical Islam, I thanked our dinner partners for how critical France has been to the United States throughout our history, even our foundation.

Our dinner guest looked at me incredulously and said, "How was that?" I replied that without the efforts of Lafayette, the American Revolution would not have been won. Tears welled in his eyes and with a broken voice he said, "20,000 dead at Normandy. Debt repaid."

What price must people be willing to pay for freedom from their oppressors? Why is it that each generation must learn this lesson again? Why are we not constantly vigilant to defend it?

The result of Germany's actions and subsequent defeat in the Second World War was the defection of many German scientists to the United States. The Soviet Union also scrambled to conscript and detain German scientists in Russia. The Arms Race was on.

Both sides took relentless steps to out-do the other. We were the first to have a working nuclear weapon. The Soviet Union was the first to send a man into outer space and bring him back alive.[cxxxix]

We developed advanced technologies in nuclear powered submarines. They caught up. They perpetually sought to overturn governments in smaller nations around the world. We sought to prop up governments that were against socialism and communism, even at the expense of defending tyrannical despots.

The Cold War was fought on many levels. James Bond romanticized undercover spies using advanced technologies in the movies, and covert operations of Special Forces were secretly being used on foreign fronts.

Throughout all of it, the enemy was recognized and understood by Americans and the Free World. The fear of nuclear annihilation drove the State Department to play a strong hand in international negotiations. The farce of the United Nations worked against the United States' (and the world's) best interests, and this piece of false theater, funded by U.S. tax dollars, was used by Liberals and Progressives and by the State Department's bureaucrats to pretend they were "preventing war."

Ultimately, President Ronald Reagan brought about the destruction of the Soviet Union. How did he do it? The threat of greater technology through laser missile defense that the Soviets could not match, and the economic strength of Reagan's policies won the Cold War. Ronald Reagan brought this about after the near destruction of our economy by the successive policies of LBJ, Richard Nixon, and Jimmy Carter, all in order to bankrupt the Union of Soviet Socialist Republics. President George Herbert Walker Bush watched the dissolution of an enemy of over 50 years.

Did you notice what brought about the victory? It was the combination of a free market economy's ability to innovate military technology through the private sector, and the prosperity that resulted from it.

NEVER FORGET: All wars, all conflicts, all "jihads" are ALWAYS ABOUT THE MONEY.

The Cold War was a horrid period of American History, one that could have been avoided if FDR and many other Progressives of his day were not sympathetic to Josef Stalin. What would have been the result if General Patton had been allowed to drive the troupes from Berlin to Moscow to stifle communism then and there? We will never know…

Today the face of the enemy has changed. Although there truly is an "axis of evil" comprised of Iran, North Korea, and Syria, those nations are small players compared to the military power of the United States. Part of the challenge with these "small players" is their support by other large nations, including Russia, China, and Pakistan.

Many nations are seeking nuclear weapons. The United Kingdom, France, Russia, China, India, Pakistan, and North Korea already hold nuclear weapons.[cxl] South Africa developed them and then disassembled them.[cxli] Israel is suspected to have nuclear weapons but has never tested them.[cxlii] Iran's desire for its own nuclear weapons poses a great threat because of the nation being controlled by Radical Islam.

Despite all this, the face of war on the earth has changed forever. We have many new and more insidious enemies. Every one of them has their own self interests at heart, and whether their objective is to destroy our nation, pillage and plunder our wealth, reduce us to the level of a Third World Nation, bring us to "justice" for how we have "raped the world," kill us as "infidels," or remove the rights of mankind that the founders of our nation (and every generation since) have paid blood to defend, they all want one thing. They seek to destroy us.

Let's take a quick look at our country's enemies, the ones who have overtly or covertly declared war against us.

Radical Islam
Radical Islam is not a "new" occurrence. The birth of "warrior Islam" goes all the way back to the 6th Century, and Mohammed's teachings. What began as a nomadic culture with hard disciplined rituals of worship and the reduction of women to the level of chattel, has become engrained in many cultures around the world. Radical Islam attempts to inflict itself on a global society in which it does not fit.

Beliefs are far more powerful than the truth. The concept that anyone who does not believe what you believe is an "infidel," deserving only death if they do not convert to Allah under the teachings of Mohammed, is a very strong childhood indoctrination. It is these radical beliefs that allow some believers to justify becoming suicide bombers among crowds of children.

More importantly, this enemy exists outside of any "nation." The strategies are long term, seeking to infiltrate nations and insisting on Sharia Law within a country's own sovereign borders. This movement "plants" people inside a nation, living as "upstanding citizens" for 10 years or more. Some of them serve in our military as witnessed by the slaughter at Fort Hood. This is not the Cold War. The enemy is hidden, the enemy does not fight on principles any other group of people have ever fought on or lived by in the history of mankind. You cannot fight this war through diplomacy, and the war cannot be won by military strength alone.

Drug Cartels
Perhaps you do not think of drug cartels as a mortal enemy of the United States. They are. Members of Mexican drug cartels have invaded U.S. National Parks in Arizona. They are armed and dangerous. Signs warn U.S. citizens not to enter the parks.[cxliii] It is bad enough that President Obama did not regard this strongly enough to send in the Armed Forces to clean out an invasion of our nation by a foreign military. What is worse is that he did not regard it as an Act of War.

Drug cartels invading the United States are bad for everyone. They are terrible for people in this country, especially for those who destroy their own lives through use of the cartels' "product." They steal money from our nation. They threaten residents and landowners and take away their ability to live in safety.

Democrats are just as culpable as the President. The Constitution plainly declares the federal government is empowered with the responsibility to "protect the general welfare." They are failing. You would think that at the rate Democrats and Progressives spend money, they would at least try to "protect their own general welfare" by throwing the IRS at the drug cartels for all the lost tax collection…

The Axis of Evil

Iran, North Korea, and Syria are our sworn enemies. North Korea has atomic weapons (thanks to China). Iran is trying to build them. A despot is leading Syria and slaughtering his own people. Beyond this Pakistan hid Osama Bin Laden, and nations in Africa are being taken over by Islamic radicals[cxliv] who destroy American Embassies[cxlv] and kill U.S. citizens.[cxlvi] These are all very real and present dangers, and attempts to counter with conventional means are not working.

The wars in Iraq and Afghanistan have taken a terrible toll, both in the lives of our soldiers and the cost of waging these wars. The State Department in many cases has worked against the advice of the military under the Obama administration. President Obama, likewise, went on a global "apology tour" for America's conduct in the world.

Cyber Terrorists

There are two elements of life in today's world that impact all aspects of our lives: Energy and Technology. They touch everything we do.

It is difficult for our enemies to completely destroy our energy systems; they just use a combination of cartels and stupidity on the part of our leadership in Washington to escalate the price of energy.

Technology is a different story. Banking could not exist without it. You could not shop, farmers could not raise crops, and schools could not operate without it. The very fundamentals of how our government, military, and communications systems are run is dependent on technology.

Cyber crime has become the "corruption du jour." Identity theft has skyrocketed because of it. Cyber terrorism is the next phase.

It is already occurring. The release of military documents though a cyber leak, access to private information in United States foreign affairs by enemy nations, even the amazing virus that infiltrated Iran's nuclear facilities are all cyber driven, and you do not beat this with guns, ships and planes.

China

Is China an enemy? Aren't they our largest trading partner and our biggest creditor? How can they be an enemy? China represents an enemy of a different kind. They represent an economic enemy.

American politicians have short life spans by Chinese standards. People in political power in the United States have to think in terms of survival every two, four or six years. The collapse of our nation's wealth, and by that its strength, is the result of politicians on both sides of the aisle, but particularly Democrats and Progressives. They squander the purpose and power of our nation through handouts. They do it to stay in office. They are drawn to staying in office because of their addiction to the power it provides them.

China is a different story. China thinks of time in 100-year blocks. As evidence of this, let's look at Hong Kong.

Global Colonialism by many European nations was rampant during the 1800s. Britain, the Netherlands, France, India and the United States saw Imperial China as the world's largest untapped market. In 1840, the British launched their first expeditionary forces to claim a rocky undeveloped island that later was known as Hong Kong.

Within a few decades, Hong Kong became a major import/export port for global trade. Through the Opium War and a series of treaties, the British were able to legitimately claim the territory until 1997.[cxlvii] A negotiated 99-year lease expired then, and China took over the largest economic portal in the Far East.

China is an enemy, but not the same kind as Mao Tse Tung was during the Cold War. They have become an economic enemy, and despite being a communist country they have become smart enough in how Capitalism really works to be "eating our lunch." They do this through manipulation of the value of their currency, protectionist trade practices our presidents have signed through the State Department and Congress,[cxlviii] and the impact of American unions (and a lack of States' "Right To Work" legislation) on our ability to compete in manufacturing.

If we do not get smarter in the global economic war, we will become the loser nation in a world we taught to prosper. China will replace us – perhaps not in four years, perhaps not in 10 years, but as we have shown through Hong Kong, they will destroy us economically. Remember, all wars ARE ALWAYS ABOUT THE MONEY.

What has to be done? What must change? How do we win a multi-fronted war that our national leaders refuse to fully address and our citizens are woefully unaware of?

We need a major change of tactics on two fronts: at the State Dept., and through the coordination of National Defense efforts.

The New Mindset of the State Department

The State Department does not change simply because each new President nominates a new Secretary of State. The few positions that change at the top of the department tend to be political in nature, and the "lifetime" positions below them know it. Ambassadors to foreign nations have traditionally been posh appointments to large campaign contributors, and the bureaucrats beneath them control the real engine of foreign affairs.

Typically, to be in a position of power in the State Department, you needed to be in that Department at least 15 to 20 years. Beliefs, tactics, and strategies are deeply engrained. Without question, the vast majority of these people are still trapped in the Cold War. Our next president must spend the first four years of his term systematically weeding out the leadership who do not understand the framework and critical urgency of our real wars. The State Department must understand they are SECONDARY to our national defense, not the foundation of it.

National Defense

The basis for our national defense must reside in the combined and cooperative efforts and assessments of the Pentagon, CIA, FBI, Homeland Security, National Guard, Coast Guard, U.S. Marshals, Secret Service, State Sheriffs, and Law Enforcement.

Currently the magnitude and size of the bureaucracy through different agencies cripple not only the efficiency of our national security, but our ability to restore and strengthen a safe America. The president must build a leadership team who will coordinate information and activity electronically and tear down the "fiefdoms" that dominate every one of these critical contributors to the safety and prosperity of our nation. There must be a "take no prisoners" approach to this change. If you get in the way, you are GONE.

Is there a precedent for this type of approach?

President Clinton forced the replacement of all 93 U.S. attorneys shortly after he took office.[cxlix] Clinton did not want U.S. attorneys who had been put into their positions by Ronald Reagan and George Herbert Walker Bush. He did it for political purposes. We must do it because of the urgency of the war against our nation.

The President and our Congress are sworn to defend the nation "against all enemies within and without." What a pity the citizens of our country have been deluded into electing Liberals and Progressives who, if not overt enemies themselves, have played into the hands of all our enemies.

Rebuilding and Refocusing National Defense and Foreign Affairs is the Fourth Rule of the Golden Way Out.

THE GOLDEN RULES OF ECONOMICS

20 THE GOLDEN WAY OUT, PART 7

The Budget

Simple facts are always the most overlooked. If you spend more than you make, you eventually will either be broke, enslaved to your creditors, or become unethical in an attempt to survive.

For all the legislative and regulatory insanity foisted upon American Citizens in the past 100 years by both parties, (but particularly Progressives, Liberals, Socialists, and Democrats), the worst of all of it could have been avoided if they had just *limited* their spending to how much money they had available in taxes. In the same way, did they really understand the impact that regulations would ultimately have on taxes?

Let us be plain. Our problems all revolve around the government's insatiable addiction to spending, and the taxes they need to pay for it.

Consider seven simple challenges with taxes:
1. The impact of taxes on the ability to generate wealth.
2. The effect of taxation on how much is actually collected in total tax revenue.
3. The impact of regulatory laws and how much their fulfillment changes total tax collection.
4. The consequences of "favored" taxation to special interests and how it changes the distribution of wealth.
5. The creeping growth of hidden taxes and how they cripple the middle and lower class.
6. The consequences of taxation of the private sector on businesses.
7. The overt lie that taxes paid by businesses are actually paid by those businesses. They are paid by consumers who cover the cost of those taxes through the items and services they purchase.

As House Budget Committee Chairman, Paul Ryan (R) of Wisconsin recently submitted a budget plan for America.[cl] While it would be easy to go through Ryan's budget line by line and compare it to any of the proposed budgets from President Obama, there are some simple truths that any federal budget has to adhere to.

Over the last 50 years the average tax revenue generated as a percentage of Gross Domestic Product (GDP) has been steady at about 18%, regardless of the tax rate.[cli] The GDP for 2011 was around $15 trillion.[clii] The Congressional Budget Office projected total tax revenue of $2.2 trillion for 2011.[cliii] The problem is our annual Federal budget is close to $3.6 trillion,[cliv] leaving a deficit of $1.4 trillion. These numbers can vary by $200 billion depending on your information source, but the point is we run a huge deficit every year.

How large is this deficit? To pay off the existing debt (assuming no additional future budget deficits) would take over $100,000 from every working age man and woman. The debt is so large that if you took 100% of the income of the top 1% of wage earners, it would not cover one year of the national budget deficit![clv]

If you increase prosperity in the private sector, the GDP goes up. When the GDP goes up, tax collection goes up (greater frequency of trades, greater frequency of tax collection). In order to eliminate the funding gap between tax revenue and spending, there are some very core changes that must take place in the budget and the economy. Paul Ryan's budget, at its core, addresses four of these issues.

Taxes

Historically the government can only expect to recover around 18% of overall GDP in tax receipts. If you increase taxes beyond the point at which the private sector can grow, the GDP goes down. The public sector (government and its bureaucrats) **DOES NOT** increase the GDP. In fact, the larger the public sector's consumption of money gets, the faster the GDP shrinks.

The only way to increase the total taxes collected is to increase GDP. This can only be accomplished by lowering the tax rate on everyone, but particularly on businesses. This puts more money in the hands of the citizens to spend, invest, or save as they see fit. Increasing the number of transactions that take place increases the number of times taxes on those transactions are collected.

Remember, every time you buy something it is an automatic tax event. From a pack of gum to a car purchase, taxes are paid. More transactions equals more taxes collected, and this in turn grows the country's GDP, which in turn makes the overall GDP pie bigger; 18% of a bigger GDP pie means more tax revenue.

Paul Ryan's budget plan cuts personal taxes from the current 35% maximum to 25%.[clvi] Ryan's budget plan also cuts corporate tax rates down to 25%, while President Obama wanted to lower the rate to 28% from the current rate of 35%.[clvii] Again the only way to get more revenue is to increase GDP.

The insidious part of Obama's so-called budget? The cost of his ever-spiraling regulatory laws impacts the cost of goods and services nearly as much as his taxation of business and individuals in the country. Isn't that great? You pay more taxes to hire more bureaucrats to create and force more regulatory laws that cost as much as the entire tax code to follow and enforce.[clviii] Fundamentally, this means that government forces trades on the private sector that are illegal to refuse. These trades are both overt and covert.

Spending Cuts

Now that you have increased the GDP you must follow this up with spending cuts. Paul Ryan's plan would cut entitlements and do away with ObamaCare. The health care bill alone could cost over $2 trillion in the next 10 years, twice as much as the American people were told it would cost.[clix]

Paul Ryan's budget plan also caps government agencies' fiscal budgets. Currently, federal agency budgets go up on average 8% per year no matter what. This increase is not tied to taxes or GDP growth. Federal agency budgets just go up.[clx clxi]

There is a simple math principle called "The Rule of 72." If you take the percentage of growth (8%) and divide it into 72 (72/8), it magically tells you the number of years (9) it will take the original value to double. What does that mean? An automatic 8% annual increase in government agency budgets means federal spending DOUBLES EVERY NINE YEARS without supervision by Congress, control by the President, or ANYTHING to do with the federal budget.

By forcing spending cuts you limit the amount of overspending Washington can do year after year.

Military Spending

President Obama's budget looked to save money by **cutting** military spending. It resulted in the threat of sequestration; forcing radical cuts without Congressional authority.

This is just a bad idea.

Conflicts in the world have changed over the years. No longer are large-scale wars fought, rather small regional conflicts and terrorist attacks are the new norm today. The world must know that any country harboring terrorists faces the strength and firepower of the U.S. armed forces. Review Chapter 19 to see the entirely new war and the multiple enemies with whom we are engaged.

The reality in today's world is that some of our enemies find it honorable to die in the fight against us. A weak Armed Forces only emboldens our enemies. The world must know and sense our might. The effect of a terrorist attack on our GDP, as well as the human cost, is just too high. The U.S. must be safe. A strong military helps to ensure this safety. More importantly, a strong U.S. military increases the strength of our overall economy. Today enemies both within and outside of our borders cripple us. They are all fighting us economically. Crushing our enemies wins the economic war. After all, **ALL** wars are about the **MONEY**.

Paul Ryan's budget **increases** military spending.[clxii] Balancing the budget should not be done on the backs of our troops. This sends the wrong message to the world.

124

Shrinking Government

Chairman Ryan's budget will shrink government. The simple act of freezing mandatory federal budget increases will, over time, shrink the federal workforce. A smaller more efficient government frees up more money for GDP growth. Doing away with ObamaCare will also help to shrink the size of our government.

Fundamentally, President Obama believed that government is the answer to the problems we face, and if we just get government running better or more efficiently we could save money and solve our problems. Obama's solution was bigger government with more oversight and regulation. The flaw in his argument is brutally being experienced in the United States today. How sad that Liberal/Progressive beliefs have emotionally captured so many Americans that they believe lies and emotions instead of 100 years of irrefutable historical proof.

It is simple to understand. Growing government takes money and resources away from businesses which in turn lowers our GDP, and creates fewer taxes collected. This prevents our government from paying its bills, which turns us into an impoverished nation in less than 5 years.

Solutions

The Ryan Budget is a great first step in getting our country on the path to fiscal freedom. The budget attempts to address four of the core principles needed to get our country moving in the right direction.

Tax reform, spending cuts, military spending and shrinking government are key steps we must take to get us moving in the right direction.

The Passing of a Budget Similar to the Paul Ryan Budget is the Fifth Rule of the Golden Way Out.

Note: My thanks to Paul Quanrud, P Revere, and Joe Henry for their contributions that helped shape this chapter.

21 THE TRUTH ABOUT WASHINGTON

People have different beliefs about Washington, DC. Some believe the leaders in the political party of their choosing are also saint-like, and are their inspiration for "hope in the goodness of our society and mankind." Some believe Washington is the nation's "universal parent," with responsibilities that include taking care of its citizens; a nanny to take care of the "nanny state." Some believe it is an "evil empire" needing to be taken down; extremists both on the left and the right hold this belief. Others believe that everyone in Washington, especially the politicians, are corrupt or at best "get corrupted" once they are there.

Everyone acknowledges that Washington, DC carries a lot of power. Very few people understand the level of power that is truly contained in the federal government and the agencies that operate as part of it.

At a minimum, Washington has control of:
- The Courts
- The Laws
- The Military
- Government trades with private companies
- Our nation's participation in global trade

The most terrifying thing that Washington has control of is something the founders of our nation fought to keep OUT of the hands of government. For many reasons, over the past 100 years, Washington has taken control of its citizens' MONEY.

Why is this so critical? What is it about money that drives all other factors of life? Is it the power in Washington that results in so many being corrupted, or is it that control of the money creates the power in Washington, DC?

What is the definition of "money"? I learned it from Miss Lehman, my 3rd grade teacher. She pointed out that our parents could not on their own build

127

the houses we lived in, grow the food we needed, create the medicines that made us better when we were sick, or even sew all the clothes we wore. Instead, each of our parents contributed things of value in life. By trading those things of value with others who needed them in exchange for the things we needed, all of us had clothes, homes, food, bicycles, and medicines. When we could not trade directly with those people who had what we needed or wanted, usually because of how far away they were, people used MONEY as a means of agreeing on the VALUE of the trade.

Simple definition?

Money is the measure of the value of any trade

When you combine this with the definition of Capitalism, *("an economic system of barter in which all the trading partners believe they receive equal or greater value in exchange for what they give up...")*, money becomes the basis for each person's well being and survival. In other words, money is the driving factor for Maslow's Hierarchy. As an adult, you cannot rise up from survival to safety to loving and belonging, to esteem and ultimately to self-actualization without sufficient money to reach survival and safety first.

Learning to manage and control money is a life lesson. Just as Capitalism is instinctive, managing and controlling money is not. It is a funny dichotomy. Trading is instinctive in mankind as a creature, but getting reasonably effective at it is not.

I believe it is the desire of nearly all people to live a life of economic security. Most people learn that it is an economic challenge to survive in today's world. Think of the cost of raising children, college tuitions, or even owning a new car. Some people have had economic security. Whether they lived in a "golden economic age" (Israel under Solomon, Babylon under Nebuchadnezzar), or try to experience it by watching TV sitcoms, everyone has a desire to live the "life of the rich and famous," or at least of the rich.

The history of mankind is mostly the opposite. Using power to take away an individual's personal control of their money is as old as the history of society. Think of monarchies and feudalism. The King was the sovereign ruler over the nation and owned most of the land. Princes, Dukes, Counts and Knights owned the rest of the land outside the cities. The Churches owned their buildings and their grounds. Merchants and craftsmen owned their goods and tools and traded their wares and skills. Most of the people were serfs. Serfs were owned by the upper class and had no rights. Life as a serf was squalid, and their value was so low that being trampled to death in the street by the upper class's galloping horses held no consequence.[clxiii]

Communism had similar consequences for its citizens. The top echelons of the Party lived lives of splendor. The few who kept control of the people through the military and police state lived what we would consider "lower middle class" lives. The rest of the population had their lives controlled by the State, including whether they could get an education, what they were allowed to believe, the type of a job they should work, and how much they were paid. No wonder alcoholism was rampant in the Soviet Union. It was the cheapest way to self-medicate out of the hopelessness of one's own existence.

Socialism has the same results. Look at the past 60 years of the nation of Greece. What was once a thriving conservative economy, the second largest commercial ship builder in the world, home to some of the wealthiest individuals in the world (Stavros George Livanos and his nephews, Aristotle Onassis and Stavros Niarchos[clxiv]), and the port for the United States Navy's 6th Fleet, fell to socialism in 1981 under Harvard educated Andreas Papandreou.[clxv]

Papandreou nationalized all privately held businesses larger than a tailor shop or taxicab. An entire generation of Socialist propaganda was perpetrated throughout the educational system. An entitlement society ensued in a country that did not use credit cards and barely used checks. Greece was, and still is, an economic system based in cash, and when your cash runs out the government is the only path to survival.

Thirty years later Greece is financially in ruins. Perhaps the most distressing part? On April 11, 2012, a 77-year-old man killed himself in the city's busy Syntagma Square in front of the Greek Parliament. He was a "self-made" entrepreneur who owned a pharmacy, probably one of the largest privately owned types of business the government allowed.[clxvi]

Greek media reported he left a suicide note accusing the government of cutting his pension to nothing. He had been investing **his own** money for retirement into the Greek pension system, the only one available to him. The collapse of their economy by decades of government corruption, overspending, and mismanagement of Greece's budget left him a choice of rummaging through trash cans to eat or ending his own life. Surely human dignity deserves more.

Today, our federal government controls more elements than you would care to discover. The bureaucracy is so entrenched that winning Conservative political candidates who come to Washington hoping to provide sound policy changes are overwhelmed by the size of the White House's control of the administration of the United States. Remember: 15 Cabinet Branches,[clxvii] 34 Czars and their departments,[clxviii] and 479 Agencies.[clxix] Add to this the unfettered growth of annual budgets combined with the current administration's addiction to unlimited entitlement programs. The federal budget pie is being cut up and sent in different sizes and flavors to all 50 states, one of which your Congressman and Senators represent.

Here is the "rub." Federal money is good for your state, isn't it? "Free" money pouring in has to help your local economy, doesn't it?

The cold hard facts? Congress can frequently be boiled down to a simple visual. Think of a horse-trading corral with billions of dollars on the line. The Representative from Utah may be willing to provide the Representative from Upstate New York his vote, IF the representative from Upstate New York offers his vote in return.

If only our financial problems were caused by legislation from the Congress! New and better legislation would fix this, and in a relatively short period of time. The real problems come from The White House and the Administration branch. Thanks to Congress and Richard Nixon, most of the federal budget goes up over 8% per year WITHOUT new spending, just through automatic budget increases.[clxx] Congress has NO say in this at all!

Even if the Administrative side of the federal budget could be controlled, it would not get us out of our financial crisis. In 2012 the Obama Administration wrote over 80,000 pages of new REGULATORY LAW.[clxxi] [clxxii] Congress had no say in any of it other than to have passed laws that ALLOWED them to do it. Add this to the existing collection of regulations and you find out a frightening fact. The cost to businesses and individuals who follow these regulatory laws is estimated at over $1 trillion per year in hourly wages for the labor.[clxxiii] Think of that number! It is an unreported "tax" of a *Trillion Dollars* that provides *little to no contribution to the economy*. It is just an expense inhaled by U.S. citizens. If there are 200 million adult American citizens, it equates to an average of $5,000 per year per person in hidden costs.

Don't get me wrong. Our nation does require a certain set of standards and guidelines to protect us. Liars, cheats, thieves, Enron and Madoff would still be stealing us blind if these were not in place. The quality of food and medicines would suffer. Insider trading and stock market manipulation would be rampant. We need regulations – just not the incomprehensible number of them that are a silent taxation on all of us.

Are you understanding HOW you are being cheated in the trade?

Most newly elected Conservative Congressmen and Senators who have not previously served in the Congress come to Washington with strong motivations to "fix" what is wrong. You elected them to do it; they arrive in DC, they meet the party leaders, the story line changes.

Whether it is facing the daunting task of tearing down the mountain that was built by 10 decades of "compromises," or lack of control a Senator or Congressman has over the President's ownership of the bureaucracy, almost nothing has slowed the growth of this horrid beast. Even the President faces an overwhelming task in breaking down and shrinking the nearly 500 agencies that ultimately report to him. We are at the day where this beast is about to eat our nation alive, and if we allow it to happen we will never recover.

How challenging is Washington? What are the most basic conflicts a financially conservative Congressman or Senator faces?

Perhaps the most distressing statement I have heard blatted out by Democrats and Progressives, and then echoed by the mainstream media, is *"We have to work together. We have to compromise. You have to 'give' a little."*

Can someone explain to me how you "compromise" when you KNOW government spending must be reduced and the other side says government spending must be increased? There IS NO COMPROMISE. Either spending goes up and the problem gets worse, or spending goes down and the solution begins.

Survival in Washington is the same as survival anywhere. The most powerful survive, usually at the expense of the weaker. New members of the Congress are the weakest. They are offered more power, but they must "compromise." Many eventually give in, hoping to achieve less than they wanted in the belief that "something is better than nothing."

How do we stop this? What can we do to end the crippling cycle in Washington and to slay the beast?

There are four key steps:

1. The ultimate power comes from being elected and then re-elected. Educated voters can hold elected officials accountable through many methods, but ultimately by being organized for electing or replacing their representatives at all levels of government.

2. The people must understand the tactics of war used by Progressives and Democrats. The people, combined with Conservative political leadership, must create a war plan that destroys the enemies of our survival.

3. We must talk in simple terms anyone can understand, and get the message out not just to like-minded people, but also to the vast majority of Americans who have been spoon-fed the talking points and embalming fluid of the Left. Most people "get it" when simple facts, irrefutable logic, and compassion for their circumstances are shared.

4. We must use all facets of 21st Century communications (Facebook, Twitter, LinkedIn, cable/satellite news, talk radio, websites, email, etc.) to reach out to the people who make up our great nation, and to overcome the bias of "mainstream" media.

And that is The Truth About Washington...

22 THE GOLDEN BAROMETER

So far we have reviewed:
- What are The "Golden Rules"?
- How they have been violated
- How we allowed that to happen
- The "Golden Way Out"
- The way Washington works

Our nation is at a point of crisis. Unless there is a dramatic change of leadership in the upcoming and following elections, the "great experiment" of a Democratic Republic will have been soundly defeated by the same types of enemies who enslaved average people in all nations for millennia. This chapter is about what all of us as citizens of the United States need to know about candidates, and how to get the right ones into office.

I think it is important to start with a clear understanding that we are engaged in war. It is the same war that founded the nation. Today we are losing that war, and if we do lose, recovery will not take place in your children's lifetime. I hope you are taking the real challenges we face very seriously. We need to mobilize the "militia" of regular people in the nation to turn the tide on this war, and hopefully, destroy the enemy forever.

The most basic rule of warfare is to know the weapons and tactics of your enemy. During the American Revolutionary War, the founders of our country were underfunded, outmanned, out-gunned, and many colonialists were NOT in favor of it. Despite these incredible obstacles, the true threat of economic enslavement drove them to find a way to win. We face the same threats today.

Look at the way Progressives/Liberals/Democrats wage their political war today.

I. Third Party Collusion - This takes place in many forms. Just a few include:

133

- Shifting Education from Teaching "How To Solve and Create" to Teaching "What To Believe"
- Mercantilism/Washington Inc. Collusion with "Chosen" Private Sector Businesses[clxxiv]
- Mainstream Media (Television, Print, Radio News, News Agencies)[clxxv]
- Union Leadership
- Unionization of Government Employees

II. Threats and Violence - These are very real and occur in a broad set of ways including:
- Protection of Liberal Radical Fringe Elements
- Covert and "Veiled" Encouragement of Violent Mob Activity (Seattle "Occupy" Group)[clxxvi]
- Economic and Personal Destruction of Anyone They Consider Dangerous
- Endless Lawsuits Against Individuals and Institutions They Consider A Threat[clxxvii]
- Collusion With Union Leadership
- Filibuster and Bribery Of Their Own In Congress To Pass Their Agenda (Obamacare in the Senate)[clxxviii]
- Eating Their Own Alive If They Do Not "Toe The Mark" (Senator Joe Lieberman)[clxxix]
- Ignoring Laws Violated By Groups Favorable To Them (Black Panthers At Election Booths 2010)[clxxx]

III. Financial Bankruptcy
- Automatic Budget Increases[clxxxi]
- Growing/Unlimited Entitlement Programs; Dependent Classes of Voters[clxxxii]
- Weakening of National Defense[clxxxiii]
- Spending Big Money Through Agencies For Political Purposes Only (USAID Tech Challenge On Atrocity Prevention)[clxxxiv]
- Nationalizing Sectors Of The Economy (Health Care)

IV. Cultural Destruction
- Class Warfare

- Shifting Education from Teaching "How To Solve and Create" to Teaching "What To Believe"
- Inciting College Students To Progressive/Liberal Support Through Emotion, Lies, and Talking Points
- Establishing Themselves As The Ruling Elite
- Seducing Republicans and Some Conservatives With "Entry" Into The Ruling Elite
- Collusion/Control of the Mainstream Media (Television, Print, Radio News, News Agencies)
- Collusion With Organizations Such As MoveOn.org Funded By George Soros[clxxxv]

V. Bureaucracy and Legislation
- Automatic Budget Increases
- Growing/Unlimited Entitlement Programs; Dependent Classes of Voters
- 15 Cabinet Agencies,[clxxxvi] 34 Czars,[clxxxvii] over 479 Federal Agencies,[clxxxviii] and hundreds of State and Local Agencies[clxxxix]
- Hiding Activity and Policy Behaviors (Eric Holder, Fast & Furious)[cxc]
- Unionizing of Government Employees
- Filibuster and Bribery Of Their Own In Congress To Pass Their Agenda (ObamaCare in The Senate)
- Eating Their Own Alive If They Do Not "Toe The Mark" (Senator Joe Lieberman)
- Spending Big Money Through Agencies For Political Purposes Only (USAID Tech Challenge On Atrocity Prevention)

VI. Messaging
- Use of Social Media[cxci]
- Collusion/Control of the Mainstream Media (Television, Print, Radio News, News Agencies)
- Hiding Activity and Policy Behaviors (Eric Holder, Fast & Furious)
- Fabrication of Agenda/Policy Issues With Conservatives (Mitt Romney is "Anti-Women," Ryan Budget Will Push Old People Over The Cliff In Health Care and Social Security)

VII. Ground Tactics
- Organizing and Driving Out The Vote On Election Day
- Blocking Voter ID[cxcii]
- Fabricating Votes and Voters[cxciii]
- Endless Lawsuits Against Individuals and Institutions They Consider A Threat[cxciv]

Conservative and rational people must find ways to *counter* this war every year. The nation has run out of time economically. If we cannot stop the financial insanity over the next four years, our country will never survive as the nation most of us believe it was created to be.

To reverse course economically, it is imperative that everyone clearly understand what all candidates in their districts believe. For this reason, I have created a **"Golden Barometer."**

The approach is simple: Rate the candidates 1 to 5 on a questionnaire about the policies and rules of the economy that must take place to save the nation. (Questionnaire and submission instructions included at the end of this chapter.)

We will post the ratings of as many national elected officials as we can. Hopefully with cooperation from each of the states we can rank officials in state office as well, including governors, state senators, and state representatives. Then anyone can visit the website at http://truecapitalism.org to find out what is going on in their own district.

Once you know who is running, we can all band together to educate our communities and drive out the votes on Election Day. There is no other hope...

THE GOLDEN BAROMETER

1. Understands the true definition of Capitalism.

   Least   Most

   1   2   3   4   5

2. Supports Legislation and Policies of Capitalism.

   Least   Most

   1   2   3   4   5

3. Understands that our current economic crisis is nothing more than an extension of the Economic War first fought during the American Revolution.

   Least   Most

   1   2   3   4   5

4. Would have fought for the patriots who founded our nation during the American Revolution.

   Least   Most

   1   2   3   4   5

5. Understands that 100 Years of Progressive Policies are the reason for our nation's current economic crisis, and that historically these policies have been put into place and allowed by both Democrats and Republicans.

   Least   Most

   1   2   3   4   5

6. Has Private Sector Career Experience, or has worked directly with the Private Sector (not Washington Inc.).

   Least   Most

   1   2   3   4   5

7. Clearly States the Economic Principles They Believe In.

   Least   Most

   1   2   3   4   5

8. Understands that the Public Sector is paid for by the Private Sector.

Least				Most
1	2	3	4	5

9. Supports the shrinking of the Federal Budget with clear policies & tactics.

Least				Most
1	2	3	4	5

10. Supports Energy Autonomy, as defined in Chapter 16.

Least				Most
1	2	3	4	5

11. Opposes "Washington Inc." (Mercantilism).

Least				Most
1	2	3	4	5

12. Will vote for the total repeal of ObamaCare.

Least				Most
1	2	3	4	5

13. Understands and will drive sound reform in National Health Care Policy.

Least				Most
1	2	3	4	5

14. Will work to create, support, and defend a balanced Federal Budget within four years of the next Congressional and Presidential term.

Least				Most
1	2	3	4	5

15. Will work relentlessly to freeze the growth of the Federal Budget outside of National Defense. Will eliminate automatic budget increases in the Federal Budget.

Least   Most

1   2   3   4   5

16. Understands that National Defense is against many new enemies, and that the basis for all our National Defense is the nation's economic sovereignty. Will work tirelessly to shift the focus of National Defense in this direction.

Least   Most

1   2   3   4   5

17. Will work fearlessly to shift our foreign policy to the protection and expansion of our country's economic sovereignty in a highly competitive global market.

Least   Most

1   2   3   4   5

18. Will create and support legislation that decreases citizens' dependency on Entitlement Programs while promoting opportunity in the Private Sector of the economy.

Least   Most

1   2   3   4   5

19. Will generate and support legislation to shrink the size and number of Federal Agencies that report both to Congress and the Administration.

Least   Most

1   2   3   4   5

20. Will fearlessly help strip down the compliance and regulatory laws that have been generated by both Congress and the Administration.

Least   Most

1   2   3   4   5

Scoring:

Just like in school, scores of 70 or lower do not pass. We need candidates who score 85 or higher on the Barometer. Check out the Golden Barometer on http://truecapitalism.org to see where your candidates for national office rank.

If you live in a district with a "failing candidate," challenge them at Town Hall Meetings, through all forms of media, and directly at their campaign offices.

If you have a candidate who is "close" to a passing grade, work with them to improve their understanding of their "weak spots."

Most importantly, reach out in your community. Visit with others, share what you have learned though this book and other sources. Get them to visit http://truecapitalism.org. Organize a "Get Out The Vote" strategy in your neighborhood or district. The hope and future of our country depends on it.

THE GOLDEN RULES OF ECONOMICS

ABOUT THE AUTHOR

Financial expert and entrepreneur **Peter Vessenes** is CEO and Founder of ProfitSee, a financial analysis and budgeting software that helps businesses manage cash flow, grow their profits and increase valuation. A nationally recognized speaker, consultant and author, Peter is also CEO and founder of Vestment Advisors, a company that helps companies of all sizes through transitions and turnarounds.

Growing up in a working-class immigrant family on the South Side of Chicago, Peter lives out the American Dream our Founding Fathers envisioned – that any success is based on hard work, personal sacrifice and merit. Sharing his lifelong entrepreneurial zeal, Peter has for over 30 years helped numerous business clients turn their businesses around and increase profits. With his business partner and wife, **Katherine,** Peter advises businesses that range from entrepreneurs to Fortune 100 corporations.

From deep concerns about the 2012 U.S. national elections, Peter's real-life experience and keen insights into government and business led him to create the American Citizens for Economic Freedom (ACEF) – a Political Action Committee dedicated to "Rebuilding the Economy One Person at a Time™ by limiting government interference in our economic freedom."

The parents of 3 children, and grandparents to three more, **Peter** and **Katherine Vessenes** reside in Shorewood, MN.

For more information:
- **ProfitSee** – www.myprofitsee.com
- **Vestment Advisors** – www.vestmentadvisors.com
- **ACEF** – http://truecapitalism.org/

THE GOLDEN RULES OF ECONOMICS

REFERENCES

[i] The Telegraph - http://www.telegraph.co.uk/news/worldnews/europe/greece/9268507/Greece-on-brink-of-collapse.html

[ii] The Economist - http://www.economist.com/node/21548229

[iiiii] Wall Street Journal - http://online.wsj.com/article/SB10001424052970204449804577068932199637016.html?mod=wsj_streaming_european-elections-may-2012

[iv] Rasmussen Reports - http://www.rasmussenreports.com/public_content/political_commentary/commentary_by_scott_rasmussen/is_the_beltway_gop_irrelevant

[v] http://www.abraham-maslow.com/m_motivation/Hierarchy_of_Needs.asp

[vi] Harry S. Truman Library and Museum - http://www.trumanlibrary.org/truman-2.htm

[vii] Encyclopedia.com - http://www.encyclopedia.com/topic/Wage_and_Price_Controls.aspx

[viii] Fox News - http://www.foxnews.com/health/2011/09/26/popular-asthma-inhaler-to-be-pulled-off-market/

[ix] In-Pharma Technologist - http://www.in-pharmatechnologist.com/Ingredients/CFC-ban-will-double-albuterol-inhaler-market-in-US

[x] AEI - http://www.aei.org/article/social-and-culture/the-secret-to-human-happiness-is-earned-success/

[xi] CNBC - http://www.cnbc.com/id/44879455/Occupy_Wall_Street_Protesters_Demand_Student_Loan_Relief

[xii] Abraham Maslow - http://www.abraham-maslow.com/m_motivation/Hierarchy_of_Needs.asp

[xiii] History Place - http://www.historyplace.com/worldwar2/triumph/tr-munich.htm

xiv Linda Hall Library - http://railroad.lindahall.org/essays/brief-history.html
xv Wall Street Journal - http://online.wsj.com/article/SB1000142405274870395970457545443 1457720188.html
xvi The Washington Times - California Democratic Party creditor in Solyndra bankruptcy http://www.washingtontimes.com/news/2011/sep/25/bankrupt-solyndras-curious-creditor/?page=all
xvii The Charlotte Observer - NLRB blocking Boeing plant construction in South Carolina http://www.charlotteobserver.com/2011/04/20/2238449/nlrb-tries-to-block-boeings-plant.html
xviii Manifesto of the Communist Party - http://www.marxists.org/archive/marx/works/1848/communist-manifesto/
xix U.S. Census Bureau - https://www.census.gov/hrd/www/jobs/incent.html
xx U.S. Office of Personnel Management - http://www.ars.usda.gov/SP2UserFiles/Place/54000000/CREEODiv ersity/Federal%20Benefits.pdf
xxi Thrift Savings Plan - https://www.tsp.gov/planparticipation/eligibility/typesOfContributio ns.shtml#agencyMatching
xxii U.S. Census Bureau - http://www.census.gov/hrd/www/benefits/fehb.html
xxiii U.S. Office of Personnel Management - http://www.opm.gov/insure/dental/index.asp
xxiv U.S. Office of Personnel Management - http://www.opm.gov/insure/vision/index.asp
xxv U.S. Office of Personnel Management - http://www.opm.gov/insure/flexible/index.asp
xxvi U.S. Office of Personnel Management - http://www.opm.gov/3rs/fact/3RS_newQAs.asp

xxvii U.S. Office of Personnel Management - http://www.opm.gov/oca/pay/studentloan/html/5CFR537.asp
xxviii PostalWork - http://postalwork.net/benefits.htm
xxix USA Today - http://www.usatoday.com/money/economy/income/2010-08-10-1Afedpay10_ST_N.htm
xxx Merit System Protection Board - http://www.mspb.org/Federal-employee-termination-procedures.html
xxxi Ibid
xxxii Lyndon Baines Johnson Library and Museum. - http://www.lbjlib.utexas.edu/johnson/archives.hom/biographys.hom/lbj_bio.asp#1960
xxxiii Compilation of U.S. Government sources - www.usgovernmentspending.com
xxxiv Ibid
xxxv U.S. Environmental Protection Agency - http://www.epa.gov/aboutepa/history/origins.html
xxxvi University of California, Berkeley - http://bancroft.berkeley.edu/ROHO/projects/debt/budgetcontrolact.html
xxxvii Congressional Budget Office - http://www.cbo.gov/doc.cfm?index=393&type=0
xxxviii Ibid
xxxix Ibid
xl Congressional Budget Office - http://www.gao.gov/special.pubs/appforum2011/scorekeeping_guidelines_2011.pdf
xli Seeking Alpha - http://seekingalpha.com/article/285091-a-look-at-who-really-owns-u-s-government-debt
xlii National Affairs - http://www.nationalaffairs.com/publications/detail/managing-the-federal-debt
xliii The New York Times - http://www.nytimes.com/2012/04/13/business/global/disappointing-italy-bond-auction-weighs-on-european-stocks.html

xliv ZeroHedge - http://www.zerohedge.com/news/its-official-total-us-debt-passes-15-trillion

xlv Wall St. Journal Online, "Where the Tax Money Is", April 17, 2011: http://online.wsj.com/article/SB10001424052748704621304576267113524583554.html This assessment uses 2008 IRS income tax statistics: 1.65 trillion deficit / 12 months = 137.5 billion shortfall per month. 938 billion revenue / 137.5 billion monthly shortfall = 6.8 months of deficit coverage by taking 100% of the taxable income from the wealthiest 1%

xlvi Federal Budget - http://www.federalbudget.com/
ZeroHedge - http://www.zerohedge.com/news/its-official-total-us-debt-passes-15-trillion
US Debt Clock - http://www.usdebtclock.org/
George Mason University - http://mercatus.org/publication/how-much-federal-spending-borrowed-every-dollar
National Priorities Project - http://nationalpriorities.org/en/publications/2011/presidents-budget-fy2012/?gclid=CPj709ePvqwCFY3KKgod9kX3qA

xlvii The Blaze - http://www.theblaze.com/stories/liberal-college-students-eager-to-redistribute-wealth-are-less-eager-to-redistribute-hard-earned-grades/

xlviii GPA Redistribution: Day 1 [Video] - www.youtube.com/watch?v=CpV9FPRQmck

xlix American Enterprise Institute - http://www.aei.org/article/politics-and-public-opinion/polls/spreading-the-wealth-isnt-fair/

l Insider Monkey - http://www.insidermonkey.com/blog/2011/11/14/congressmen-get-pass-on-insider-trading-reports-60-minutes/

li California Watch - http://californiawatch.org/dailyreport/white-house-knew-solyndras-condition-obamas-visit-13588

lii Washington Times - http://www.washingtontimes.com/news/2011/sep/25/bankrupt-solyndras-curious-creditor/

liii Political Jack - http://www.politicaljack.com/forums/showthread.php?7239-80-of-%91Green-Energy%92-Loans-Went-to-Obama%92s-Top-Donors

liv The Daily Beast - http://www.thedailybeast.com/newsweek/2011/11/13/how-obama-s-alternative-energy-programs-became-green-graft.html

lv Throw Them All Out: Peter Schweizer, *Throw Them All Out*, Houghton Mifflin Harcourt Publishing Co., New York, 2011.

[lvi] Kellogg School of Management, Northwestern University - http://www.kellogg.northwestern.edu/News_Articles/2009/galinsky_research.aspx
[lvii] National Priorities Project - http://nationalpriorities.org/en/budget-basics/federal-budget-101/spending/
[lviii] Congressional Research Service - http://www.fas.org/sgp/crs/misc/R41681.pdf

[lix] George Mason University - http://mercatus.org/publication/state-and-local-governments-outpace-growth-private-sector
[lx] American Rhetoric - http://www.americanrhetoric.com/speeches/dwightdeisenhowerfarewell.html
[lxi] U.S. Department of Energy - http://energy.gov/articles/obama-administration-offers-535-million-loan-guarantee-solyndra-inc
[lxii] Federal Register - http://www.gpo.gov/fdsys/pkg/FR-2011-01-03/pdf/FR-2011-01-03.pdf
[lxiii] Federal Register - http://www.gpo.gov/fdsys/pkg/FR-2011-12-30/pdf/FR-2011-12-30.pdf
[lxiv] Who Is A Progressive? - http://teachingamericanhistory.org/library/index.asp?document=1199
[lxv] Lecture - http://www.youtube.com/watch?v=hHG6vc6gCSc
[lxvi] U.S. Department of Education - http://www2.ed.gov/about/overview/fed/role.html
[lxvii] FDR American Heritage Center - http://www.fdrheritage.org/new_deal.htm
[lxviii] U.S. History - http://www.ushistory.org/us/56e.asp
[lxix] U.S. Department of Energy - http://www.lm.doe.gov/land/sites/oh/fernald_orig/aboutfernald/dhist.htm
[lxx] U.S. Department of Education - http://www2.ed.gov/about/overview/fed/role.html
[lxxi] FY 2011 HHS Budget in Brief (pdf) p.1 as numbered http://www.hhs.gov/about/budget/fy2011/#Brief

[lxxii] FY 2011 DOE Agency Financial Report (pdf) pp.4-5,17 as numbered http://energy.gov/about-us/budget-performance

[lxxiii] U.S. Department of Education - http://www2.ed.gov/about/overview/budget/index.html

[lxxiv] U.S. Environmental Protection Agency - http://www.epa.gov/planandbudget/results.html

[lxxv] USA Today - http://www.usatoday.com/news/nation/2010-03-04-federal-pay_N.htm

[lxxvi] Despair, Inc. - http://www.despair.com/government.html

[lxxvii] Thomas J. DiLorenzo, *How Capitalism Saved America* (New York: Three Rivers Press, 2004), p. 54.

[lxxviii] Thomas J. DiLorenzo, *How Capitalism Saved America* (New York: Three Rivers Press, 2004), p. 54, 55

[lxxix] Thomas J. DiLorenzo, *How Capitalism Saved America* (New York: Three Rivers Press, 2004), p. 55

[lxxx] Thomas J. DiLorenzo, *How Capitalism Saved America* (New York: Three Rivers Press, 2004), p. 55 - 57

[lxxxi] Downsizing the Federal Government - http://www.downsizinggovernment.org/agriculture/food-subsidies

[lxxxii] The College Conservative - http://thecollegeconservative.com/2011/12/13/my-time-at-walmart-why-we-need-serious-welfare-reform/

[lxxxiii] Sen. Mike Carrell - http://senatormikecarrell.blogspot.com/2011/03/committee-approves-my-bill-to-police.html

[lxxxiv] Washington State Legislature - http://apps.leg.wa.gov/billinfo/summary.aspx?bill=5877&year=2011

[lxxxv] Big Government - http://biggovernment.com/sberry/2011/12/08/connecticut-state-employees-fraudulently-filed-for-food-stamp-benefits/

[lxxxvi] U.S. Economic History Since 1945, Michael French, Pages 137, 138 http://books.google.com/books?id=Tzq8AAAAIAAJ&pg=PA137&lpg=PA137&dq=Regulated+industries+in+the+USA+1950s&source=bl&ots=P9qv3SvQr7&sig=KXh2SONFTTulmBF0mJPDI44Tyz0&hl

=en&sa=X&ei=m4BJT-
PxN5GGsgLL84jrCA&sqi=2&ved=0CEMQ6AEwBA#v=onepage&q
=Regulated%20industries%20in%20the%20USA%201950s&f=false
lxxxvii Economic History Association -
http://eh.net/encyclopedia/article/castaneda.gas.industry.us
lxxxviii Interstate Commerce Commission -
http://www.encyclopedia.com/topic/Interstate_Commerce_Commissi
on.aspx
lxxxix Living History-
http://www.livinghistoryfarm.org/farminginthe30s/water_11.html
xc U.S. Food and Drug Administration -
http://www.fda.gov/RegulatoryInformation/Legislation/FederalFood
DrugandCosmeticActFDCAct/default.htm
xci Bureau of Alcohol, Tobacco, Firearms, and Explosives -
http://www.atf.gov/press/releases/2008/12/122908-historical-
badges-tell-story.html
xcii Patricia Martin and David Weaver. "Social Security: A Program and
Policy History." Page 7.
xciii The Cuban Missile Crisis: Timeline -
http://library.thinkquest.org/11046/days/timeline.html
xciv Encyclopedia of Business and Finance -
http://www.enotes.com/balance-trade-reference/balance-trade-
174121

xcv U.S. Energy Information Administration, 4-Week Avg U.S. Net
Imports of Crude Oil and Petroleum Products (Thousands Barrels per
Day) -
http://www.eia.gov/dnav/pet/hist/LeafHandler.ashx?n=PET&s=WT
TNTUS2&f=4
xcvi Making the Case for ANWR -
http://www.anwr.org/Background/Making-the-case-for-ANWR.php
Congressional Research Service; U.S. Oil Imports and Exports -
http://www.fas.org/sgp/crs/misc/R42465.pdf

xcvii New York Stock Exchange - http://www.nyse.tv/crude-oil-price-history.htm

xcviii U.S. Department of Labor, Bureau of Labor Statistics - http://www.bls.gov/news.release/empsit.t15.htm

xcix Centers for Disease Control, United States Life Tables, 2004 pg. 35 http://www.cdc.gov/nchs/data/nvsr/nvsr56/nvsr56_09.pdf

c Centers for Disease Control 2011 - http://www.cdc.gov/nchs/data/hus/2011/022.pdf

United State Census 2012 - http://www.census.gov/compendia/statab/cats/births_deaths_marriages_divorces.html

ci Actuarial Life Table - http://www.ssa.gov/oact/STATS/table4c6.html

cii The Incidental Economist - http://theincidentaleconomist.com/wordpress/what-makes-the-us-health-care-system-so-expensive---conclusion/

ciii 2011 Milliman Medical Index - http://insight.milliman.com/article.php?cntid=7628?&utm_campaign=Milliman%20Homepage&utm_source=milliman&utm_medium=web&utm_term=home%20banner&utm_content=MMI

civ Ibid

cv Bureau of Labor Statistics-Consumer Price Index - http://www.bls.gov/schedule/archives/cpi_nr.htm

cvi 2011 Milliman Medical Index, p. 3 - http://publications.milliman.com/periodicals/mmi/pdfs/milliman-medical-index-2011.pdf

cvii The Heartland Institute-Understanding Rising Hospital Inpatient Costs: Key Components of Cost and The Impact of Poor Quality - http://heartland.org/policy-documents/understanding-rising-hospital-inpatient-costs-key-components-cost-and-impact-poor-q

cviii General Accounting Office-Medical Malpractice Insurance Multiple Factors Have Contributed to Increased Premium Rates - http://www.gao.gov/new.items/d03702.pdf

cix PricewaterhouseCoopers - http://www.pwc.com/us/en/healthcare/publications/the-price-of-excess.jhtml

cx Ibid

cxi 2011 Milliman Medical Index - http://insight.milliman.com/article.php?cntid=7628?&utm_campaign =Milliman%20Homepage&utm_source=milliman&utm_medium=web &utm_term=home%20banner&utm_content=MMI

cxii Ibid

cxiii U.S. News - http://www.usnews.com/news/washington-whispers/articles/2011/04/07/6-pages-of-obamacare-equals-429-pages-of-regulations

cxiv The Heartland Institute-The ObamaCare Disaster - http://heartland.org/policy-documents/obamacare-disaster

cxv Copeland, Curtis W, *New Entities Created Pursuant to the Patient Protection and Affordable Care Act*, Congressional Research Service. July 8, 2010 https://www.aamc.org/download/133856/data/crsentities.pdf.pdf

cxvi Ibid

cxvii Patient Protection and Affordable Care Act, Section 6301 and 6302 http://www.ncsl.org/documents/health/ppaca-consolidated.pdf

cxviii Congressional Budget Office-CBO and JCT's Estimates of the Effects of the Affordable Care Act on the Number of People Obtaining Employment-Based Health Insurance - http://www.cbo.gov/publication/43082

cxix Letter from Douglas Elmendorf, director, Congressional Budget Office, to House Speaker Nancy Pelosi, March 20, 2010 http://cbo.gov/sites/default/files/cbofiles/ftpdocs/113xx/doc11379 /amendreconprop.pdf

cxx Budget Committee Republicans - http://www.roadmap.republicans.budget.house.gov/UploadedFiles/R oadmap2Final2.pdf

cxxi Centers for Medicare and Medicaid Services – NHE summary including share of GDP, CY 1960-2010 - https://www.cms.gov/Research-Statistics-Data-and-

Systems/Statistics-Trends-and-
Reports/NationalHealthExpendData/NationalHealthAccountsHistorical.html
[cxxii] Centers for Medicare and Medicaid Services - https://www.cms.gov/Research-
Statistics-Data-and-Systems/Statistics-Trends-and-
Reports/NationalHealthExpendData/Downloads/proj2010.pdf
[cxxiii] Wall Street Journal -
http://online.wsj.com/article/SB1000142405297020474090457719535
2148844134.html
[cxxiv] ZeroHedge - http://www.zerohedge.com/news/us-closes-2011-
record-1522-trillion-debt-officially-1003-debtgdp
[cxxv] Reuters - http://www.reuters.com/article/2010/06/08/us-usa-
treasury-debt-idUSTRE65765820100608
[cxxvi] The Daily Caller - http://dailycaller.com/2012/03/30/another-17-
trillion-surprise-found-in-obamacare/
[cxxvii] ZeroHedge - http://www.zerohedge.com/news/massive-17-
trillion-hole-found-obamacare
[cxxviii] CBS D.C. – http://washington.cbslocal.com/2012/03/27/you-
can-make-people-buy-broccoli-scalia-goes-after-health-care-law/
[cxxix] Wall Street Journal -
http://online.wsj.com/article/SB1000142405270230472440457729176
2007718228.html
[cxxx] GoodQuotes.com -
http://www.goodquotes.com/quote/alexander-hamilton/it-s-not-
tyranny-we-desire-it-s-a-just
[cxxxi] tipping point. (n.d.). Collins English Dictionary - Complete &
Unabridged 10th Edition. Retrieved April 01, 2012, from
Dictionary.com website:
http://dictionary.reference.com/browse/tipping+point
[cxxxii] The White House Cabinet -
http://www.whitehouse.gov/administration/cabinet
[cxxxiii] Front Page Magazine -
http://frontpagemag.com/2011/05/16/obama%E2%80%99s-czars-
and-their-left-wing-affiliations/
[cxxxiv] Index of U.S. Government Departments and Agencies -
http://www.usa.gov/directory/federal/index.shtml

cxxxv State and Local Government Agencies -
http://www.usa.gov/Agencies/State-and-Territories/Agencies-by-Topic.shtml
cxxxvi The Free Dictionary -
http://www.thefreedictionary.com/bureaucrat
cxxxvii Transcript of the Constitution of the United States -
http://www.archives.gov/exhibits/charters/constitution_transcript.html
cxxxviii Government Spending as a Percentage of GDP -
http://www.ritholtz.com/blog/2011/07/government-spending-as-a-percentage-of-gdp-2/
cxxxix Slate -
http://www.slate.com/articles/news_and_politics/the_gist/1997/09/russians_in_space.html
cxl Federation of American Scientists-Status of World Nuclear Forces -
http://www.fas.org/programs/ssp/nukes/nuclearweapons/nukestatus.html
cxli International Atomic Energy Agency (IAEA) National Report-Nuclear verification in South Africa -
http://www.iaea.org/Publications/Magazines/Bulletin/Bull371/37105394248.pdf
cxlii Federation of American Scientists-Nuclear Weapons -
http://www.fas.org/nuke/guide/israel/nuke/

cxliii Borderland Beat -
http://www.borderlandbeat.com/2010/06/pinal-county-sheriff-mexican-drug.html
cxliv The Globe and Mail -
http://www.theglobeandmail.com/news/world/world-view/spectre-of-danger-looms-over-possible-intervention-in-mali/article4267452/
cxlv Reuters - http://www.reuters.com/article/2012/06/06/us-libya-attack-us-idUSBRE8550GX20120606

[cxlvi] Time - http://www.time.com/time/world/article/0,8599,1670883,00.html
[cxlvii] CNN World - http://edition.cnn.com/2002/WORLD/asiapcf/east/06/20/hk.history.01/
[cxlviii] Cato Institute - http://www.cato.org/publications/free-trade-bulletin/trade-policy-priority-one-averting-uschina-trade-war
[cxlix] The Washington Post (reposted on HighBeam Research) - http://www.highbeam.com/doc/1P2-938837.html
[cl] The Path to Prosperity - http://budget.house.gov/uploadedfiles/pathtoprosperity2013.pdf
[cli] The Real Tax Rate Conundrum - http://www.zerohedge.com/print/446236
[clii] Bureau of Economic Analysis - http://www.bea.gov/newsreleases/national/gdp/gdpnewsrelease.htm
[cliii] Congressional Budget Office - http://www.cbo.gov/publication/21999
[cliv] New York Times - http://www.nytimes.com/interactive/2010/02/01/us/budget.html
[clv] Wall Street Journal - http://online.wsj.com/article/SB10001424052748704621304576267113524583554.html
[clvi] Reuters - http://blogs.reuters.com/talesfromthetrail/2011/04/13/obama-vs-ryan-how-the-deficit-plans-compare/
[clvii] Washington Post - http://www.washingtonpost.com/business/economy/obama-to-propose-lowering-corporate-tax-rate-to-28-percent/2012/02/22/gIQA1sjdSR_story.html
[clviii] The Impact of Regulatory Costs on Small Firms - http://archive.sba.gov/advo/research/rs371tot.pdf
[clix] The Real Cost of ObamaCare - http://news.investors.com/article/522147/201002241922/the-real-cost-of-obamacare.htm

clx Heritage Foundation – Federal Budget in Pictures -
http://www.heritage.org/budgetchartbook/mandatory-discretionary-spending

clxi House Votes to Eliminate Automatic Spending Increases -
http://cnsnews.com/news/article/house-votes-eliminate-automatic-spending-increases-budget

clxii The Path to Prosperity -
http://budget.house.gov/uploadedfiles/pathtoprosperity2013.pdf

clxiii Feudalism Pyramid - http://www.middle-ages.org.uk/feudalism-pyramid.htm

clxiv CNN Money -
http://money.cnn.com/magazines/fortune/fortune_archive/1992/09/07/76826/index.htm

clxv Andreas G. Papandreou Foundation -
http://www.agp.gr/agp/content/Document.aspx?d=7&rd=5499005&f=1403&rf=1842884619&m=4728&rm=11934981&l=1

clxvi British Hellenic Chamber of Commerce -
http://www.bhcc.gr/en/useful-info/introgr

clxvii The White House Cabinet -
http://www.whitehouse.gov/administration/cabinet

clxviii Front Page Magazine -
http://frontpagemag.com/2011/05/16/obama's-czars-and-their-left-wing-affiliations/2/

clxix Index of U.S. Government Departments and Agencies -
http://www.usa.gov/directory/federal/index.shtml

clxx Congressional Budget Office -
http://www.cbo.gov/doc.cfm?index=393&type=0

clxxi Federal Register - http://www.gpo.gov/fdsys/pkg/FR-2011-01-03/pdf/FR-2011-01-03.pdf

clxxii Federal Register - http://www.gpo.gov/fdsys/pkg/FR-2011-12-30/pdf/FR-2011-12-30.pdf

clxxiii The Impact of Regulatory Costs on Small Firms -
http://archive.sba.gov/advo/research/rs371tot.pdf

clxxiv Department of Energy - http://energy.gov/articles/obama-administration-offers-535-million-loan-guarantee-solyndra-inc

clxxv UCLA Newsroom - http://newsroom.ucla.edu/portal/ucla/Media-Bias-Is-Real-Finds-UCLA-6664.aspx

clxxvi CBS News - http://www.cbsnews.com/video/watch/?id=7407256n

clxxvii Breitbart - http://www.breitbart.com/Big-Government/2012/04/21/irs-harassment-of-tea-party-groups

clxxviii Fox News - http://www.foxnews.com/politics/2009/12/20/nelson-accused-selling-vote-health-nebraska-pay/

clxxix Politico - http://www.politico.com/news/stories/1209/30627.html

clxxx The Washington Times - http://www.washingtontimes.com/news/2010/jun/25/inside-the-black-panther-case-anger-ignorance-and-/

clxxxi Congressional Budget Office - http://www.cbo.gov/doc.cfm?index=393&type=0

clxxxii The Heritage Foundation - http://www.heritage.org/research/reports/2012/02/2012-index-of-dependence-on-government

clxxxiii U.S. Department of Defense - http://www.defense.gov/speeches/speech.aspx?speechid=1643

clxxxiv MSNBC - http://www.msnbc.msn.com/id/47231309/ns/technology_and_science-science/t/how-tech-can-help-prevent-violence/#.T91cBY5t1FI

clxxxv MoveOn.org - http://www.moveon.org/event/faq/index.html?faq_id=131&show_to_pic=1035&q_expand=3609#active

clxxxvi The White House - http://www.whitehouse.gov/administration/cabinet

clxxxvii FrontPage - http://frontpagemag.com/2011/05/16/obama's-czars-and-their-left-wing-affiliations/

clxxxviii USA.gov - http://www.usa.gov/directory/federal/index.shtml

[clxxxix] USA.gov - http://www.usa.gov/Agencies/State-and-Territories/Agencies-by-Topic.shtml
[cxc] Committee on Oversight & Government Reform-Operation Fast and Furious - http://issues.oversight.house.gov/fastandfurious/
[cxci] The New York Times - http://www.nytimes.com/2008/11/10/business/media/10carr.html
[cxcii] Politico - http://www.politico.com/news/stories/0412/75681.html
[cxciii] Townhall - http://townhall.com/tipsheet/katiepavlich/2012/01/11/in_new_hampshire_dead_democrats_get_to_vote
[cxcivcxciv] Breitbart - http://www.breitbart.com/Big-Government/2012/04/21/irs-harassment-of-tea-party-groups

Additional Resources:

National Debt Awareness Center - http://www.federalbudget.com/
http://www.usdebtclock.org/
George Mason University - http://mercatus.org/publication/how-much-federal-spending-borrowed-every-dollar
National Priorities Project -
http://nationalpriorities.org/en/publications/2011/presidents-budget-fy2012/?gclid=CPj709ePvqwCFY3KKgod9kX3qA

www.ingramcontent.com/pod-product-compliance
Lightning Source LLC
Chambersburg PA
CBHW070011300526
45794CB00001B/286